Contents

"The future belongs to those who believe in the beauty of their dreams."

— Eleanor Roosevelt

1. Opening the Cosmic Curtain: A Prelude to Extraordinary Journeys

Welcome to a world where the line between imagination and reality blurs, inviting you on a journey that transcends the confines of our terrestrial existence. In this book, we will explore the enthralling possibilities of intergalactic travel through the fascinating concepts of Stargates and Sidereal Subways. While these notions may seem the realm of science fiction, advancements in our understanding of space-time physics and quantum technology suggest that our universe may be far more accessible than we've ever dared to dream. Join me as we embark on an expedition not just across space, but through the very fabric of reality itself. Whether you are a seasoned cosmologist or a curious traveler of ideas, this book aims to shed light on the realities, the potential, and the future of traversing the vast expanses between the stars.

2. The Dawn of Cosmic Imagination

2.1. From Myth to Theory

Journeying through the cosmos has long been a theme woven into the fabric of human culture, from the ancient tales of gods and celestial beings to the intricate theories proposed by modern physicists. Our current understanding of intergalactic travel is a tapestry colored by myth, imagination, and empirical research, each thread contributing to our quest for knowledge about the stars. This subchapter delves into the evolution of ideas surrounding space travel, the significant transition from mythological narratives to theoretical paradigms that challenge our understanding of what is possible.

The narrative of interstellar travel commenced in the minds of our ancestors, who gazed up at the night sky, crafting stories that explained their world. Myths served not only as entertainment but also as frameworks through which ancient peoples interpreted the cosmos. These legends spoke of gods traversing the heavens, celestial chariots, and astral gates, alluding to the tantalizing possibility of movement beyond the earthly realm. The Egyptians had their ferryman, Ra, who would journey through the night sky, while the ancient Greeks spoke of the gods ascending to Olympus, traversing the very fabric of the universe. These archetypes and stories set the groundwork for future generations to ponder the boundaries of existence, hinting that perhaps travel among the stars was not just a dream but an attainable reality.

As centuries passed, these mythological constructs began to mingle with early scientific inquiry, gradually shifting the cultural perception of the cosmos from mystical to empirical. The Renaissance epitomized this transformation, as thinkers like Copernicus and Galileo challenged the geocentric model of the universe. They placed man within a broader cosmic tableau, inviting a fresh discourse on the possibility of life beyond Earth and, encouraging contemplation on how one might reach the stars. This period saw the emergence of the first speculative ideas regarding space travel, with individuals contemplating the practicality of reaching these celestial destinations.

The 20th century marked a significant inflection point in this journey from myth to theory. With the advent of modern physics, particularly Einstein's theories of relativity, the imagination of scientists was set ablaze. Here we embraced the notion of space-time as a dynamic continuum, intertwining the dimensions of time and space into a single, fluid tapestry. The implications of this revelation were seismic, paving the way for concepts like wormholes—hypothetical passages through space-time that could potentially connect distant regions of the universe. These theories illustrated that intergalactic travel might not depend solely on technology but on a deeper understanding of the universe's fabric itself.

Wormholes, once relegated to the annals of science fiction, became serious subjects of mathematical study and discussion. The speculative nature of these theories gave rise to a new domain of inquiry: the exploration of traversable wormholes and their potential applications for space travel. Researchers began to postulate that if such structures could exist, they would constitute a shortcut between two points in space, thereby enabling rapid travel across vast cosmic distances. This shift from mythological interpretation to theoretical exploration represented a watershed moment in humanity's understanding of space travel.

As technological advancements continued, the relationship between myth and science further evolved. The works of Arthur C. Clarke and other science fiction writers captured the imagination, prompting both the general public and scientists to consider the possibilities of extraterrestrial exploration and intergalactic travel. The line separating reality from fiction began to dissolve, challenging our conception of the cosmos as merely a backdrop to human existence. The themes explored in literature offered a glimpse into a future where advanced technology allowed for the exploration of regions of space previously thought unreachable. By intertwining myth and scientific advancement, authors laid the groundwork for theoretical exploration to become more expansive and daring.

Further examination of interstellar travel concepts yields a recognition of human ambition, curiosity, and the innate desire to traverse the unknown. This dynamic interplay between myth and theory is pivotal; while myth illuminated our aspirational trajectories into the cosmos, the theoretical frameworks developed by scientists grounded our ambitions within plausible scientific principles. The synthesis of narrative and empirical study rendered the dream of stargates and sidereal subways not just fanciful imaginings but rather concepts worthy of scientific inquiry and potential validation.

In conclusion, the continuum from myth to theory chronicles humanity's evolving relationship with the cosmos. As we transition into an era defined by potential advancements in technology and our understanding of space-time physics, we celebrate the legacy of our mythological ancestors, recognizing the value of imagination in catalyzing inquiry and innovation. What our forebears conceived as ethereal dreams of cosmic escapade has now transformed into a legitimate area of theoretical study—a testament to our unyielding quest to not merely gaze at the stars, but to explore them as active participants in the universe. The watery bridge of this journey, from ancient myths to contemporary theories, illuminates our intrinsic longing to uncover the mysteries of existence and invites us to dream even bigger as we stand at the precipice of possibility.

2.2. Science Fiction and Its Impact

Throughout history, science fiction has served as both a mirror and a catalyst for our understanding and aspirations concerning interstellar travel. This literary genre, allowing for boundless creativity, has provided a fertile ground for ideas that explore the possibilities of traveling across the cosmos. While also delivering fantastical narratives that often stretch the limits of scientific feasibility, science fiction has profoundly shaped public imagination and scientific inquiry, raising questions about our place in the universe, the nature of existence, and the future of humanity.

A hallmark of science fiction is its ability to envision technological advancements that far exceed current capabilities. Classic works such as H.G. Wells' "The War of the Worlds" and Arthur C. Clarke's "2001: A Space Odyssey" not only entertain but challenge us to rethink our understanding of space travel and the potential realities that may lie within it. Wells, in particular, prompted readers to consider the implications of extraterrestrial encounters, igniting a dialogue about other forms of life in the universe and the prospect of interplanetary conflict. Clarke expanded on these themes, placing human explorers on the brink of encountering profound technologies, inviting reflections on our readiness to reach out beyond our earthly sphere.

As science fiction emerged as a powerful genre, its practical impact on scientific research became increasingly evident. Authors like Isaac Asimov and Philip K. Dick illuminated pathways of thought that inspired real-world advancements in technology and space exploration. Asimov, through his "Foundation" series, posited notions of psychohistory, envisioning a future where mathematics might predict societal trends with profound accuracy. This idea not only captured the imagination of readers but has inspired a range of predictive modeling techniques across various scientific disciplines.

Moreover, seminal works detailing travel through wormholes, such as Kip Thorne's "The Science of Interstellar," translated theoretical physics into digestible narratives. Thorne's engaging explanations helped demystify complex concepts, raising public awareness about the potential for wormholes as shortcuts through space-time. This intersection between scientific theory and science fiction allowed the broader community to engage with advanced physics in an approachable manner, spurring both interest and inquiry into what was previously regarded as purely speculative.

The visceral experiences depicted in science fiction narratives also serve to cultivate a longing and ambition within audiences to explore the stars. Generations have grown up influenced by the likes of "Star Trek," which showcased the spirit of exploration and diplomacy among various species, demonstrating that travel among the stars can promote understanding and solidarity rather than conflict. The show's portrayal of the United Federation of Planets can be seen as a parallel to contemporary discussions surrounding global cooperation to address issues like climate change, emphasizing that humanity's future may indeed necessitate collaboration beyond our own world.

Another significant impact of science fiction on our understanding of interstellar travel lies in its exploration of the challenges inherent in such ventures. Works like Kim Stanley Robinson's "Mars Trilogy" take a hard look at the practicalities of colonization, introducing readers to the complexities surrounding human adaptation to new environments, societal structures, and ethical considerations of altering alien ecosystems. By approaching both the promises and pitfalls of interstellar colonization, science fiction not only entertains but educates readers about the responsibility that comes with exploration.

The genre's imaginative freedom allows exploration of dystopian futures, presenting cautionary tales around unchecked technological advancement and the potential consequences of humanity's reach exceeding its grasp. For instance, in Octavia Butler's "Parable of the Sower," readers encounter a society profoundly shaped by climate change and social upheaval, forcing them to reckon with the implications of neglecting our planet. This highlights the need for a balanced approach as we consider the future of space travel, urging both scientific advancement and ethical stewardship.

Moreover, science fiction has often provided a framework for exploring the philosophical ramifications of interstellar travel. Writers delve into themes of identity, consciousness, and the concept of the "other," prompting a re-evaluation of what it means to be human in an interconnected cosmos. The exploration of different forms of life poses essential questions: How will we define sentience? What ethical obligations do we owe to other beings? What impact will interstellar travel have on our understanding of consciousness?

As technological advancements bring us closer to the feasibility of intergalactic travel, the legacy of science fiction becomes increasingly apparent. It serves as both a guide and a warning, as the genre continually pushes the boundaries of what we believe is possible. The myriad of ideas proposed within its narratives have inspired scientific research, generated public interest, and sparked invaluable discourse.

In conclusion, science fiction has become an indispensable force in shaping our aspirations for interstellar travel. Its impact is not confined to fiction alone; it permeates our societal consciousness, engaging our imaginations while providing a foundation upon which future scientific inquiry may be built. As we stand at the threshold of potential advancements that could transform theoretical concepts into reality, we must be mindful of the narratives we continue to cultivate. The vastness of space beckons us not only to dream but to approach our explorations with a sense of responsibility for ourselves, other beings, and the universe as a whole. As we chart our course forward, we are reminded that science fiction is not merely a portal to fantastical worlds but also a powerful motivator for real-world progress in our journey among the stars.

2.3. Early Philosophical Thoughts

In the earliest stages of human thought, the cosmos represented more than a mere backdrop for terrestrial existence; it was a realm of profound philosophical inquiry. Long before empirical science began to shape our understanding of the stars, thinkers and dreamers alike gazed upward, pondering the nature of reality and our place within its vastness. This subchapter delves into the philosophical frameworks that emerged from humanity's fascination with the cosmos, focusing specifically on early thoughts surrounding possible travel beyond our Earthly confines.

Ancient civilizations, infused with a sense of wonder, conceived the universe as a dynamic interplay between the divine and the mundane. In many cultures, the heavens were thought to be populated by a pantheon of gods and celestial entities, each exerting influence over human affairs and natural phenomena. The Mesopotamians and Egyptians, for example, developed intricate cosmologies that placed the sun, moon, and stars at the center of their spiritual and philosophical beliefs. Ra, the sun god of Egypt, symbolized rebirth and the cycle of life; his nightly journey through the underworld sparked contemplations of an afterlife and the transcendence of the human spirit beyond physical boundaries.

As philosophy progressed into classical antiquity, thinkers such as Plato and Aristotle introduced more systematic approaches to understanding the cosmos. Plato's "Timaeus," written in the 4th century BCE, presented a vision of the universe as an ordered whole, governed by a rational principle. He speculated about the possibility of celestial travel, envisaging a harmonious cosmos in which each star and planet held meaning and purpose. This philosophical inquiry illuminated a budding recognition that humanity might not only observe the stars but also aspire to reach them.

Aristotle expanded upon Plato's ideas with his empirical approach, categorizing celestial bodies and arguing for their natural properties. He viewed the heavens as unchanging and perfect, leading him to dismiss the possibility of travel beyond the Earth. For Aristotle, the stars were fixed entities, forever beyond reach. However, it was this very contradiction—of longing for the unreachable—that ignited the hearts of subsequent thinkers and dreamers, paving the way for a philosophical discourse on the nature of space and existence.

Fast forward to the Renaissance, a critical paradigm shift occurred that transformed philosophical thought into a burgeoning scientific inquiry. The revolution ignited by Copernicus' heliocentrism reframed humanity's perspective of the cosmos, reorienting Earth from the center to a moving planet, orbiting the sun among many. This monumental shift reshaped philosophical musings surrounding human existence. If Earth could no longer be considered the universal fulcrum, what then lay among the stars? The intellectual freedom of this era allowed thinkers like Galileo and Kepler to explore the mathematics and mechanisms of celestial movements, igniting a passion for discovery and laying the groundwork for future explorations of the heavens.

In contemplating the vastness of space, philosophers began to wrestle with questions around the nature of existence and the implications of travel beyond our world. René Descartes, in the 17th century, proposed a dualistic view of the mind and body, which led to later inquiries surrounding the conception of consciousness in outer-space contexts. If technological advancement enabled humanity to transcend physical confines, what would that mean for the essence of human identity? Descartes' reflections would ripple through the ages, influencing the philosophical exploration of consciousness and ultimately inspiring considerations of sentient life beyond Earth.

As exploration of the cosmos continued to unfold, philosophers of the Enlightenment era scrutinized humanity's motivations for seeking other worlds. Figures like Immanuel Kant engaged deeply with the implications of the infinite, asserting that the pursuit of knowledge was an innate human drive compelling us to venture into the stars. Kant framed the desire for exploration as a quest for understanding the sublime, intertwining the emotional and intellectual pursuits of humanity with the philosophical desire to engage with the cosmos beyond.

With the dawn of the 20th century and the emergence of modern science, the realms of philosophy and physics began to intermingle in unprecedented ways. Theoretical physicists like Albert Einstein reshaped notions of time and space, challenging the absolute nature of existence and inviting deeper philosophical questions about the very fabric of reality. The implications of relativity suggested that the universe was malleable; space and time were not mere stage settings but actively interconnected dimensions that could potentially allow for interstellar travel. This prompted philosophical speculation regarding the implications of traversing the universe—would crossing distances redefine our understanding of identity, existence, and the very nature of life?

Moreover, thinkers like Martin Heidegger framed inquiries into existence itself by emphasizing the interplay of Time, Being, and human experience. His musings inspired contemplations on the nature of journeys—both physical and metaphorical—and the consciousness that accompanies them. If humanity could breach the limits of what we know, what transformations would accompany our newfound freedoms? Heidegger's work thus intertwined with the ever-growing discourse on the ethical dimensions of cosmic exploration, engaging with the potential consequences of intergalactic travel.

As we transition into the present and beyond, the philosophical discourses of early thinkers serve as anchors in our exploration of intergalactic travel. The intertwining threads of myth, metaphysics, and scientific inquiry represent a rich tapestry that informs our modern understanding of the cosmos—each question posed adds depth and dimension to our pursuit of knowledge. This reflection on early philosophical thoughts ultimately elucidates the profound human desire to rekindle connections with the stars. As we stand poised at the precipice of potential exploration, it becomes evident that our earlier musings remain integral to harnessing the future implications of stargates and sidereal subways. In seeking to traverse the vast expanses of the universe, we are not merely pursuing the act of movement; rather, we are embarking on an odyssey marked by a rich philosophical legacy that guides and inspires our journey beyond the bounds of Earth.

2.4. Astronomy Through the Ages

In the grand tapestry of human history, the stars have always loomed large, kindling a sense of wonder that has driven our collective curiosity since time immemorial. Astronomy, the scientific study of celestial bodies and the universe, has persistently reshaped our understanding of space—its vastness, intricacies, and eventual accessibility. The evolution of astronomy illustrates a progression from rudimentary observations rooted in early civilization to advanced scientific principles capable of predicting what lies beyond our terrestrial confines. This journey through the ages not only chronicles our discoveries about the cosmos but also reflects the changing paradigms in humanity's view of itself and its place within the universe.

In the early epochs of human history, astronomical knowledge was predominantly intertwined with mythology and religion. Ancient civilizations, such as the Babylonians and Mayans, meticulously charted the movements of celestial bodies, linking them to agricultural cycles and human affairs. Their observations were often governed by a dualistic approach; while the cosmos was a source of awe and spiritual significance, it was also critical for the practicalities of daily life. The appearance of certain stars signaled the time for planting and harvesting, thus knitting the heavens into the fabric of human survival and cultural practices.

As these civilizations flourished, they developed increasingly sophisticated astronomical frameworks. The Greeks, for instance, introduced geometry and mathematical reasoning into astronomical inquiry. Philosophers such as Aristarchus of Samos proposed ideas about the heliocentric model—where the Earth revolved around the sun—centuries before Copernicus would later monumentalize this concept. They initiated the critical thinking that prompted scientific questioning, illustrating that celestial observations could transcend mere superstition and become objects of rational study. By establishing foundational astronomical practices using mathematics and observation, these early thinkers set the stage for future exploration into the nature of the cosmos.

The transition from ancient mythos to empirical observation became most pronounced during the Renaissance. The invention of the telescope by Galileo Galilei marked a paradigm shift, allowing for unprecedented observations of the universe. Galileo's telescopic discoveries, including moons orbiting Jupiter and the phases of Venus, challenged long-held beliefs about the universe's structure and humanity's place in it. His advocacy of a heliocentric model sparked a revolution, laying the groundwork for modern astronomy by affirming the use of observation, experimentation, and evidence in scientific pursuits. As scientific inquiry gained momentum, so did the sense of intellectual liberation; humanity began to see itself as an integral part of a vast and dynamic cosmos, rather than the exalted center of a divinely ordered universe.

The subsequent centuries witnessed further rapid advancements in astronomical understanding. Isaac Newton's formulation of the laws of motion and universal gravitation not only unified the heavens and Earth but also established a theoretical framework that explained celestial movements through mathematical laws. Newton's work propelled humanity toward grasping not just the mechanics of the celestial bodies but also a more profound comprehension of the nature of space and time itself. The implications of his theories were immense, leading to developments in navigation and contributing to the Age of Exploration. By the 19th century, astronomy had burgeoned as a discipline, cultivating a generation of astronomers who relentlessly surveyed the sky and expanded the catalog of known celestial objects.

The dawn of the 20th century heralded yet another metamorphosis in our understanding of the universe thanks to the work of pioneers like Albert Einstein. His theories of relativity redefined the conceptual frameworks of space and time, suggesting that the universe is an intricate and interconnected tapestry rather than a static void. With the advent of quantum mechanics, scientists were grappling not only with the macroscopic cosmos but also with the strange and counterintuitive behaviors of particles on a minuscule scale. These advancements prompted humanity to reconsider not just how we look at space but also how we think about our role in an ever-expanding and changing universe.

As astronomy progressed into the modern era, the development of technology took center stage. Telescopes grew in power and sophistication, and satellites began to probe the deepest corners of our solar system and beyond, vastly increasing our knowledge of celestial phenomena. The advent of radio astronomy opened new avenues of exploration, allowing scientists to detect celestial radio waves that reveal the activity of some of the universe's most energetic events. The ability to observe cosmic background radiation provided vital evidence of the Big Bang, marking a watershed moment in our understanding of the universe's origins.

In the later decades of the 20th and early 21st centuries, advanced computing and imaging technology spurred on observational astronomy, enabling previously unfathomable insights into the structure and evolution of the cosmos. The rise of space telescopes like the Hubble Space Telescope allowed us to capture stunning images of distant galaxies and celestial phenomena, prompting profound philosophical reflections on our place in an almost unfathomably large universe. The discoveries of exoplanets orbiting distant stars have provoked tantalizing questions about the potential for extraterrestrial life, prompting humanity to envision itself as part of a larger cosmic community.

Simultaneously, these advancements in astronomy and the growing body of theoretical knowledge have invigorated the concept of intergalactic travel. As our understanding of the universe deepens, the idea of traversing cosmic distances transforms from mere fantasy into a legitimate field of scientific inquiry. The exploration of ideas surrounding wormholes, time dilation, and quantum entanglement suggests that intergalactic travel, once confined to the realms of science fiction, is increasingly a topic worthy of exploration and understanding within theoretical physics.

The implications of all these astronomical advancements reverberate through the broader narrative of human existence. Each astronomical discovery has not only altered our scientific understanding but has also shaped our cultural consciousness, influencing literature, art, and philosophy. Our evolving relationship with the cosmos reflects a core aspect of the human experience—a yearning to connect, to explore, and to expand our horizons in the face of the unknown. The quest for knowledge fuels our imaginations and propels us into the future, with an eye toward not just observing the stars but exploring what lies beyond them.

In conclusion, astronomy has traversed an awe-inspiring arc from its mythological roots to a sophisticated scientific discipline capable of hypothesizing intergalactic travel. The continuous dialogue between observation, theory, and technology underscores humanity's unrelenting urge to comprehend its place in a vast cosmos. As we stand on the precipice of potential intergalactic travel with the concepts of Stargates and Sidereal Subways, we find ourselves at a moment ripe with possibilities, driven by a legacy of inquiry that has defined our relationship with the universe. The journey of astronomy reflects a microcosm of humanity's larger narrative—a story of discovery, ambition, and the perpetual quest to become more than we are, fueled by an unshakeable desire to reach for the stars and beyond.

2.5. The First Concepts of Wormholes

The exploration of wormholes, a concept that has tantalized scientists and the public alike, finds its roots deeply embedded in the theoretical foundations of physics. Wormholes are hypothesized structures that could act as shortcuts through space and time, potentially enabling travel between distant points in the universe. This idea prompts a reevaluation of our current understandings of the cosmos and offers hopeful insights into the mechanics of intergalactic travel.

The journey into the theoretical constructs of wormholes begins with the groundbreaking work of Albert Einstein and Nathan Rosen, who, in 1935, presented what is now famously known as the Einstein-Rosen bridge. This term refers to a theoretical model that describes a solution to Einstein's equations of General Relativity, suggesting a bridge-like connection between two separate points in space-time. Scientific curiosity was piqued by the implications of their work; if these connections, or bridges, could exist, they might serve as conduits for instantaneous travel across vast cosmic distances. The Einstein-Rosen bridge suggests a profound interconnectedness between regions of space that would otherwise be separated by enormous distances, fundamentally transforming our approach to the universe.

The implications of these theories were not immediately embraced; for many years, wormholes remained a mathematical curiosity with limited experimental validation. However, as thinkers delved deeper into the constructs of relativity and quantum physics, new pathways of inquiry revealed possibilities that could redefine our interpretations of travel and connectivity across the stars. With exploration into the realm of quantum mechanics, the notion of wormholes gained further traction. Quantum physics, featuring principles of uncertainty and entanglement, lent a peculiar dimension to the conversation around space travel; it was a realm where the oddities of the universe would challenge humanity's fundamental notions of locality and distance.

One of the vital facets of wormhole theory lies in its position within the broader fabric of space-time. The traditional view of space as a flat, unyielding plane morphed into a dynamic tapestry where gravitational forces shape the very pathways we traverse. This understanding necessitated a reinterpretation of how we perceive the universe's structure. If the fabric of space-time could be warped or curved, as Einstein postulated, then the potential for shortcuts—like wormholes—emerged as a promising frontier for exploration.

In parallel, the philosophical implications of wormholes unfolded within the scientific community as researchers began grappling with the nature of realities that could be connected by such structures. Aspects of time travel and parallel universes arose, presenting further complexities regarding causality and alternate timelines. This engagement with theoretical physics ignited imaginations and inspired speculative discussions regarding the feasibility of creating a traversable wormhole—a dichotomy of fantasy and burgeoning scientific endeavor that continues to capture the public's imagination.

The contemporary discourse around wormholes has also intersected with the fields of astrophysics and cosmology. Researchers have begun to analyze the potential manifestations of these concepts within the cosmos. For instance, specific types of astronomical phenomena —such as black holes—have emerged as focal points for exploration. Some theoretical models suggest that a black hole's event horizon could serve as the entrance to a wormhole, offering an intellectually stimulating yet elusive entry point into further investigative studies. The nature of these objects raises critical questions about the mechanics of traversing such structures safely, promoting discussions around the challenges and risks associated with this kind of travel.

Additionally, advances in observational technology have transformed our understanding of cosmic structures. Gravitational waves, predicted by Einstein's General Relativity and first detected in 2015, provide unprecedented insights into the dynamics of massive astrophysical objects. Theories around the existence of wormholes could potentially align with observable phenomena associated with gravitational waves, suggesting that the foundations of our universe harbor far more complexities than previously recognized.

In summary, the concepts of wormholes bridge a myriad of disciplinary boundaries, calling upon insights from physics, mathematics, and cosmology to construct a coherent vision of potential intergalactic travel. Emerging from speculative mathematics and theoretical physics, these ideas evolve from mere thought experiments into possibilities worthy of serious consideration. The implications of such structures—if they exist—extend well beyond travel, inviting us to reflect on the nature of connectivity, existence, and reality itself. As scientists delve further into the mysteries of the universe, the exploration of wormholes symbolizes a bold leap into uncharted territories, encompassing humanity's enduring quest for knowledge and adventure. This ongoing inquiry could catalyze the transformation of prevailing paradigms, reshaping how we understand the cosmos and our place within it in ways that continue to elude the limits of our imagination.

3. Unlocking the Stargate: Theoretical Foundations

3.1. The Einstein-Rosen Bridge

The realm of intergalactic travel has long captured the imagination of scientists, science fiction writers, and the general populace alike, with concepts such as wormholes representing some of the most tantalizing possibilities. At the forefront of these captivating ideas lies the Einstein-Rosen bridge, an elegant theoretical construct that emerged from the groundbreaking work of physicists Albert Einstein and Nathan Rosen in the 1930s. This subchapter will delve deep into the foundational principles surrounding the Einstein-Rosen bridge, its implications for intergalactic travel, the discourse it inspired within the scientific community, and the intersections of theory and practicality surrounding wormholes.

The Einstein-Rosen bridge originated from the quantifiable framework of Einstein's General Theory of Relativity, which offers a robust description of how gravity operates within the fabric of space-time. Simplistically put, the theory asserts that massive objects, such as stars and planets, warp the dimensions of space that surround them. This curvature of space-time results in the familiar experience of gravity, dictating how celestial bodies interact with one another. In their paper published in 1935, Einstein and Rosen postulated that it might be possible for these warps in space-time to create passages, akin to bridges, connecting disparate regions of the universe.

These theoretical constructs suggested that, if such passages could exist, they would serve as shortcuts—allowing for instantaneous travel between two distant points in space-time. This captivating idea drastically reconfigured our understanding of the universe, moving it from a vast array of isolated celestial bodies to an interconnected web of potential pathways that could facilitate travel and communication across astronomical distances.

While the initial response to the concept of the Einstein-Rosen bridge was largely speculative, it nonetheless ignited significant scientific curiosity. Researchers began to explore the mathematical underpinnings of the bridge, evaluating stability conditions and the potential realities of traversability. However, several fundamental questions loomed large: What would be required to create or sustain such a bridge? Would traversable wormholes collapse upon the approach of matter, or could they indeed serve as viable conduits for travel?

Further investigation revealed a considerable hurdle: any theoretical wormhole, such as that of the Einstein-Rosen bridge, required the existence of exotic matter—hypothetical materials or energetic states with negative energy density. This requirement posed conundrums, as our understanding of physics at the time offered no known means of acquiring or utilizing exotic matter. Such uncertainty tempered excitement within the scientific community, relegating the notion of traversable wormholes primarily to speculative realms, but the seeds of inquiry had been firmly planted.

Even as theorists grappled with the paradoxes of traversable wormholes, the implications of the Einstein-Rosen bridge began to weave their way into broader discussions within quantum mechanics. For instance, the bridge's potential relationship with quantum entanglement—a phenomenon where particles can instantaneously influence each other regardless of the distance separating them—suggested a new layer of complexity to our understanding of both travel and communication across the cosmos. This relationship posited tantalizing questions: If wormholes indeed conveyed connections, could they simultaneously bridge the multitude of realities inherent in a multiverse, as suggested by some interpretations of quantum physics?

The dialogue surrounding wormholes found itself woven into the fabric of contemporary physics, questioning humanity's very understanding of connectivity in a universe defined by spaces and distances. Such multifaceted conversations drew upon the experiences of people contemplating philosophical implications surrounding existence, reality, and the nature of the cosmos itself. As theoretical physicists, mathematicians, and philosophers engaged in this active discourse, it gradually became apparent that these entities could also serve as a bridge between the fictional realms of science fiction narratives and the ever-evolving landscape of scientific inquiry.

Since their introduction, the exploration of the Einstein-Rosen bridge has intertwined with various astrological inquiries about the universe's structure. The robust dynamics of black holes—regions in space characterized by extreme gravitational pull—began to provoke curiosity about whether these entities could initiate or sustain wormholes. Researchers have theorized that black holes may possess gravitational characteristics that could facilitate traversable wormholes, further emphasizing the need for more sophisticated models encompassing the behaviors of these extreme environments within the folds of space-time.

Despite the challenges, the exploration of the Einstein-Rosen bridge, and wormholes in general, has fostered innovative experimental approaches. The detection of gravitational waves—ripples in space-time produced by catastrophic astronomical events such as colliding black holes—reaffirmed some of the fundamental predictions made by General Relativity. While purely speculative, gravitational wave observations provide an invaluable avenue for probing the dimensions of the cosmos, broadening the potential understanding of phenomena that may bear resemblance to wormhole dynamics.

Ultimately, the Einstein-Rosen bridge serves as a gravitational fulcrum between desire and limitation—a theoretical pillar that embodies humanity's insatiable thirst for exploration and understanding. The questions that arise when examining the principles surrounding wormholes extend beyond mere travel; they invoke fundamental inquiries about our position in the universe, the nature of existence, and the mechanisms that unite us amid seeming isolation in the cosmos.

As we navigate this fascinating terrain, the interplay of elegance and complexity within theoretical physics reminds us that the path toward comprehending the universe is intertwined with anticipation. The Einstein-Rosen bridge represents a glimpse into the profound possibilities of what the universe may hold—a nexus of hope and inquiry, beckoning us to imagine how intergalactic travel could evolve, transforming once-distant dreams into attainable realities. The journey through the realms of intergalactic exploration is not simply a matter of traversing physical space but rather a voyage that intertwines destiny, imagination, and the exploration of the unknown.

3.2. Quantum Physics and the Multiverse

The exploration of quantum physics and the multiverse presents a fascinating intersection with the concepts of stargates and intergalactic travel, fundamentally altering our understanding of reality itself. As foundational theories of quantum mechanics have evolved, they have opened the door to unprecedented implications regarding the nature of the universe, potentially affirming the existence of pathways that transcend the limitations of space and time. By delving into the nuances of quantum theory, we might uncover the frameworks through which stargates could exist and the multitude of realities they might connect.

At the heart of quantum mechanics lies the principle of superposition, which asserts that particles can exist in multiple states simultaneously until observed. This phenomenon introduces a radical departure from classical physics, suggesting that rather than a singular, linear trajectory, particles and their behaviors form a complex web of possibilities. When applied to the concept of intergalactic travel, this principle posits that multiple paths could be navigated concurrently through various configurations of space-time—an idea that aligns seamlessly with the notion of stargates.

Moreover, quantum entanglement—the phenomenon whereby particles become interlinked to allow instant communication regardless of distance—mirrors the conceptual foundations of stargates as conduits between distant parts of the universe. Such entangled relationships suggest that connections across vast distances may be possible at levels previously thought unattainable. If stargates could facilitate travel based on quantum entangled states, they could serve as gateways between parallel realities, potentially allowing individuals to traverse not merely across the universe but across divergent timelines and dimensions. This could mean that a traveler utilizing a stargate might not only visit distant star systems but could leap into alternate universes, each governed by different physical laws or histories.

Expanding upon the implications of the multiverse theory, numerous interpretations propose that our universe is only one of countless others coexisting in a vast landscape of alternate realities. Some of these theories arise from the configuration of quantum mechanics, particularly Hugh Everett's Many-Worlds Interpretation, which posits that every time a quantum event occurs, the universe splits, creating separate branches of possibility. Such a framework suggests the existence of infinite parallel dimensions in which varied outcomes exist simultaneously. Within this tapestry of multiple realities, the possibility of traveling through stargates connecting different universes becomes tantalizingly viable. Travelers could access alternate versions of Earth, explore civilizations that might have evolved differently, or experience the diverse manifestations of the cosmos themselves.

The notion of traversing stargates to enter different realities transcends a mere technical aspect of travel; it invokes deep philosophical inquiries about identity, experience, and consequence. If travel among the stars opens pathways to alternate realities, how do we define the self and our history? Does interaction with these alternate versions of our existence alter our understanding of fate, free will, or destiny? These profound questions remain ripe for exploration within both scientific inquiry and humanity's collective imagination, as they challenge the very fabric of what it means to exist in a multiverse.

Additionally, quantum tunneling—the phenomenon whereby particles can transition through energy barriers rather than going over them—offers a striking parallel to the concept of stargates. This process not only illustrates the potential ease with which particles navigate difficult pathways, but it also invites imagination concerning how a theoretical stargate might operate. If a stargate could manifest similarly to quantum tunneling dynamics, the act of entering a stargate might facilitate traversal across vast cosmic distances, enabling travel from one point in the universe to another as seamlessly as a particle slipping through barriers.

Furthermore, as our understanding of quantum physics continues to evolve, so too does the possibility of harnessing these principles for practical application within our pursuits of exploration. Integrated into technological innovations, quantum computing and information could redefine capabilities related to intergalactic travel mechanisms and navigational systems within hypothetical stargate constructions. By leveraging the foundational physics that govern quantum behavior, we could envision a future where stargates not only function theoretically but are also intimately interwoven with the underlying principles of our universe, embodying the marriage of profound science and exploratory ambition.

In summary, the interplay between quantum physics and the multiverse offers a rich reservoir of possibilities that propel the concepts of stargates and intergalactic travel beyond the limits of conventional understanding. With principles such as superposition, entanglement, and tunneling serving as crucial foundations, we could embark on journeys that not only traverse the cosmos but also explore alternate realities and timelines. As we stand on the brink of such extraordinary possibilities, the investigation of quantum interactions and their implications deepens our excitement and provides a tantalizing glimpse of what intergalactic travel might entail in an all-encompassing multiverse. The road ahead remains marked by uncertainty and discovery, inviting humanity to dream not only of the stars but of multitude realms waiting to be explored.

3.3. Space-time Fabric and Relativity

Understanding the nature of space-time and how stargates could function within it bridges the realms of physics and cosmology, intertwining our very conception of reality. At its core, the framework of space-time, as proposed by Albert Einstein, transforms our understanding of the universe from a static expanse into a dynamic, flexible fabric—a tapestry woven with the threads of time and space that bend, flex, and warp in the presence of mass and energy.

In our conventional experience, we perceive both space and time as independent entities. We view the world in three dimensions (length, width, and height) and treat time as a singular, linear progression. However, Einstein's theory posits that these dimensions are not disparate; rather, they are interconnected facets of a singular continuum known as space-time. This radical shift in perspective has profound implications for our understanding of cosmic phenomena, including those that may facilitate intergalactic travel through mechanisms like stargates.

Central to the concept of space-time is the idea that massive objects —such as planets, stars, and galaxies—warp the fabric of the universe around them. This curvature not only affects how objects move through space but also influences how time is experienced. An object in a strong gravitational field, for example, experiences time more slowly than one in a weaker field, a phenomenon known as time dilation. This realization leads to the possibility that if we were to manipulate the fabric of space-time itself, we could potentially create conduits, or stargates, that facilitate travel across vast cosmic distances instantaneously.

In envisioning how stargates might function, we draw upon theoretical constructs such as wormholes—hypothetical tunnels within the space-time continuum that connect disparate points in the universe. Formulated initially through the equations of General Relativity, wormholes would, in theory, allow for travel that circumvents the traditional constraints dictated by the speed of light. By traversing a wormhole, an individual may enter one end and emerge at another point in space-time, effectively reducing the journey's span from light-years to mere moments.

A key aspect of stargate functionality involves the existence of exotic matter—hypothetical materials that possess negative energy density. Theoretically, exotic matter could be harnessed to stabilize a traversable wormhole, preventing the collapse that would otherwise occur upon the entrance of mass. This requirement sparks an intersection of theoretical speculation and the constraints of known physics;

while contemporary understanding of matter and energy does not yet recognize the substantiated existence of exotic matter, ongoing inquiries into quantum physics may reveal new forms of matter that could fulfill these requirements.

Within the broader philosophical and scientific discourse about stargates lies the question of how the manipulation of space-time might impact the practicalities of intergalactic travel. Considerations include not just the feasibility of creating a stable portal through which a traveler could sail, but also how this process would address fundamental concerns ranging from energy consumption to the ethical implications of crossing celestial thresholds.

As we peer deeper into the cosmic fabric, we encounter the concept of gravitational lensing, which provides compelling insights into the nature of space-time and its malleability. Gravitational lensing occurs when a massive object, such as a galaxy or black hole, bends the path of light from more distant sources due to its gravitational field. This phenomenon allows astronomers to observe objects and celestial events that would otherwise be obscured, while simultaneously providing tangible evidence of the interaction between mass and the curvature of space-time. By studying these gravitational warps, we develop a more nuanced understanding of the universe's structure, one that underpins notions of how stargates could potentially operate.

Furthermore, the exploration of time itself within the context of intergalactic travel challenges our traditional notions of causality and existence. If stargates enabled travel through time and space, they could lead to scenarios where one could encounter past or future versions of places, raising questions about the implications of returning to a time long gone or interacting with historical events. The ability to bend reality in such fundamental ways necessitates ongoing scrutiny into the ethical ramifications of such capabilities, emphasizing the need for thoughtful discourse on what it means for our understanding of existence.

In conclusion, the fabric of space-time, intertwined with relativity, offers both a theoretical and practical framework through which ideas of stargates can be explored. By comprehending the interactions between mass, energy, and the continuum, we inch closer toward envisioning a reality in which intergalactic travel becomes plausible —limited only by our understanding and exploration of the universe itself. As scientific inquiry continues to advance, the concept of stargates transcends mere imagination and emerges as a focal point for human aspirations and ambitions, reflecting an innate desire to connect with the cosmos and traverse the vast unknown that lies beyond the stars.

3.4. Gravitational Lensing as a Precursor

Gravitational lensing, an awe-inspiring phenomenon where the path of light is bent by the gravitational field of massive objects, plays a critical role in enhancing our understanding of the cosmos. This extraordinary effect not only unveils the intricate architecture of the universe but also serves as a tantalizing precursor to the development of technologies that may one day facilitate intergalactic travel through constructs like stargates.

The foundation of gravitational lensing is rooted in Einstein's General Theory of Relativity, which posits that mass can warp the fabric of space-time. When light from a distant source—such as a galaxy or a quasar—passes near a massive object (for example, a galaxy cluster), the gravitational field of that object bends the light's trajectory, creating multiple images or arcs of the source. This bending effect can magnify distant celestial objects, allowing astronomers to observe phenomena that would have otherwise gone unseen or unobservable due to their considerable distance from Earth.

Gravitational lensing serves as a powerful tool in astrophysics for studying the universe's large-scale structure. By meticulously analyzing the light patterns created by lensing effects, astronomers can infer the mass distribution of the lensing object. This has profound implications, particularly concerning dark matter—a mysterious form of matter that does not emit, absorb, or reflect light and is thus invisible by conventional means. The influence of dark matter on gravitational lensing sheds light on its abundance in the universe, assisting researchers in piecing together the puzzle of cosmic evolution.

The study of gravitational lensing has yielded significant insights into the nature of the universe, including the expansion rate of the universe and the distribution of galaxies. Such knowledge can foster the potential development of technology related to intergalactic travel, as it may offer clues about cosmic roadmaps outlined by massive structures acting as gravitational lenses. Understanding how these lenses can magnify and reveal distant cosmic phenomena presents an allegorical bridge between our current knowledge and the ambition of traversing intergalactic distances.

Additionally, lensing indicates that the universe may contain vast networks of gravitational fields that can warp time and space. Such discoveries may provide theoretical understandings and frameworks for stargate construction, which relies on manipulating the fabric of space-time to facilitate instantaneous travel. If we can envision a universe where gravitational interactions create natural pathways, we may discern how to harness and replicate these mechanisms.

The fascinating aspects of gravitational lensing raise questions about the feasibility of creating artificial structures or technologies capable of producing similar lensing effects. For example, harnessing the principles behind gravitational lenses could enable scientists to engineer localized space-time warps that function as gateways to distant regions of the universe. The implications for travel utilizing such pathways would be profound, suggesting that the manipulation of gravity could yield shortcuts across cosmic expanses.

Moreover, gravitational lensing could afford opportunities for experimenting with softening the light barrier that presents a fundamental challenge in intergalactic travel. By examining how light behaves in the presence of massive objects, researchers could expand their understanding of ways to mitigate the effects that restrict the speed and capacity of space travel. This exploration into light manipulation opens avenues for theoretical frameworks that could enable stargates or alternative travel mechanisms to facilitate access to unreachable regions of the cosmos.

The continuance of gravitational lensing research could also yield new insights into energy requirements for intergalactic travel. As we look to harness the energies of celestial bodies, understanding how gravity can bend light and influence energy patterns in the cosmos offers parallels to discovering methods to create stargates that draw upon these cosmic energy sources. Coupling astronomical observations with theoretical physics paves the way for future advancements that could deeply inform the practical logistics of operating stargates or similar technologies.

In essence, the study of gravitational lensing acts as a harbinger for intergalactic travel, presenting a roadmap toward understanding the complexities of the universe's structure and the dynamics of light. As astronomers and physicists continue to decipher the relationships between mass, light, and the fabric of space-time, they unlock not only a richer comprehension of cosmic phenomena but also the possibility of crafting mechanisms for traversing the vast cosmic highways.

Ultimately, gravitational lensing stands at the intersection of observational science and speculative inquiry, embodying the quest to transform theoretical concepts into tangible realities. As this profound phenomenon enhances our understanding of the universe, it lays essential groundwork toward the possible realization of intergalactic travel technologies—confirming that the journey beyond the stars is not just a distant ambition but a pursuit alive with potential, illuminated by the bending light of celestial marvels.

3.5. Energy Requirements for Stargate Operation

The operation of stargates, proposed as the most advanced means of intergalactic travel, hinges significantly on the energy requirements necessary to create, stabilize, and maintain these complex structures. Theoretical exploration of stargates has opened myriad questions regarding the types and quantities of energy that would be essential for their function, compelling us to examine the principles of physics that govern these celestial constructions.

At the heart of the discourse on energy requirements is the concept of mass-energy equivalence, epitomized by Einstein's famous formula: $E=mc^2$. This principle suggests that mass can be converted into energy and vice versa, implying that vast amounts of energy could potentially be harnessed if one were to manipulate matter at fundamental levels. For stargates, the energy needed would not only pertain to the creation of the gate itself but also to the energy consumption during operation—the requisite energy to open, stabilize, and facilitate travel through the structure.

One of the most compelling sources of energy for stargate operation centers around the notion of exotic matter. Exotic matter is hypothesized as a form of material that carries negative mass or energy density. This theoretical substance plays a crucial role in crafting a traversable wormhole, often depicted as a "bridge" connecting two disparate points in space-time. It is the stability provided by exotic matter that prevents the collapse of the wormhole, allowing safe passage for matter—including travelers—instead of experiencing the chaos of gravitational forces. The challenge lies in the fact that exotic matter has yet to be discovered or realized within our current understanding of physics. Thus, sourcing, producing, or synthesizing exotic matter represents a monumental task requiring energy levels that surpass anything available with today's technology.

An intriguing avenue of inquiry involves linking stargate energy requirements to energetic celestial phenomena such as supernovae or the processes surrounding black holes. Both supernovae —the explosive deaths of massive stars—and black holes, with their intense gravitational fields, represent scenarios within which staggering amounts of energy are exchanged and transformed. Harnessing energy from such high-energy events could provide the necessary fuel for creating stargates. Theoretically, if technology could be developed to tap into these cosmic powerhouses, the energy harnessed might sufficiently allow for the stabilization and operational management of a stargate.

Moreover, concepts derived from quantum physics propose that the manipulation of quantum fields could yield energy sources suitable for stargate operation. Quantum field theory describes the vacuum of space as not entirely empty but teeming with fluctuating energy levels. If techniques could be developed to draw upon this vacuum energy, they might provide the necessary fuel to open and maintain a stargate. In this vein, energy extraction from the quantum vacuum would represent an innovative leap in harnessing cosmic energy to achieve interstellar travel.

Next, one must also consider the entropic cost of stargate operation. Every system experiences entropy, which in a broader sense implies that energy conversions are never perfectly efficient. Energy losses due to heat and other forms of dissipation during the stargate operation would further elevate the energy requirements, necessitating an increase in the initial input of energy to maintain functional integrity.

Our exploration naturally leads to the viability of deploying advanced technologies to meet these energy demands. The use of fusion reactors, drawing on the power of nuclear fusion—the process that powers our sun—could represent one of the more practical energy sources available. Such reactors would operate by combining atomic nuclei to release energy, a mechanism that, while drawing on significant engineering techniques, may ultimately yield the sustainable energy output that stargate systems require.

Concepts such as artificial intelligence (AI) also emerge as pivotal components in managing energy resources during stargate operation. Sophisticated AI systems could analyze and optimize energy consumption, ensuring that the necessities for operating a stargate align seamlessly with the energy being generated or harvested within the framework of the technology.

Additionally, societal implications arise from such ambitious endeavors. The quest for harnessing vast amounts of energy raises the question—who controls this energy? The manipulation of energy sources at such magnitudes carries implications for geopolitics, economic power structures, and environmental considerations on Earth. Thus, as humanity progresses toward the possibility of stargate travel, the need for ethical governance and oversight becomes paramount, ensuring that the power cultivated is utilized responsibly and equitably.

In summary, exploring the energy requirements for stargate operation is a multidimensional undertaking that spans theoretical physics, cosmology, and societal discourse. From exotic matter to cosmic powerhouses and quantum fields, numerous speculative avenues arise as potential sources of energy needed to create and maintain these theoretical constructs. Understanding and addressing these energy demands encapsulates both the promise of advanced intergalactic travel and the responsibilities entailed in harnessing the extraordinary potentials that lie within the cosmos. As we stand on the cusp of discovering more about the universe and our capabilities within it, the journey toward unlocking the secrets of stargate operation remains both a scientific odyssey and a profound reflection of our aspirations to transcend earthly limitations and journey among the stars.

4. Sidereal Subways: The Concept of Cosmic Highways

4.1. Hyperspace and Superstring Theory

The exploration of hyperspace and superstring theory opens a doorway into speculative realms that stretch beyond our conventional understanding of space-time, potentially unveiling shortcuts that could revolutionize intergalactic travel. These concepts suggest that our universe may harbor hidden pathways and dimensions, allowing us to traverse cosmic distances far more swiftly than previously thought possible. Through an in-depth examination of hyperspace and superstring theory, we can begin to grasp the theoretical foundations of what might one day facilitate travel through stargates.

Hyperspace, in a broad sense, refers to the idea of additional spatial dimensions beyond the familiar three of length, width, and height. This notion gained traction in both theoretical physics and science fiction as researchers sought to understand how the complexities of the universe could be reconciled with the limitations imposed by traditional space-time. Hyperspace posits that if one could access these higher dimensions, it might be possible to create shortcuts through conventional space-time, allowing for rapid travel between distant points in the universe.

The origins of this idea can be traced back to the principles outlined by General Relativity, but it was further expanded through the lens of advanced theoretical frameworks, including superstring theory. Superstring theory posits that the fundamental particles constituting matter are not point-like objects but rather tiny, vibrating strings. These strings exist in a multi-dimensional universe that encompasses up to eleven dimensions, depending on the theory. Within this multi-dimensional space, strings can vibrate in different modes, leading to the emergence of various particle types and fundamental forces.

By integrating the concepts of hyperspace with superstring theory, scientists suggest that the universe is far more intricate than our traditional models of physics would lead us to believe. They propose that if we could manipulate the properties of these strings and access the additional dimensions, we could navigate through hyperspace, bypassing the restrictions of conventional travel. This new approach challenges our understanding of time and distance, offering tantalizing possibilities for traveling across vast interstellar distances with minimal time expenditure.

One of the most appealing prospects of hyperspace travel is the idea that this could be achieved through engineering devices that alter the fabric of space-time itself. By creating a localized space-time bubble or warp, akin to the theoretical constructions of a warp drive, spacecraft could be propelled through higher dimensions, effectively shortening the distance between two points in ordinary space. The concept of a warp drive remains highly speculative, yet it serves as a gateway to imagining the technological possibilities that harness the principles of hyperspace.

In the context of intergalactic travel, the implications of using hyperspace to traverse vast distances become even more profound. Instead of relying on traditional propulsion systems that are constrained by the speed of light, spacecraft designed to operate within hyperspace could navigate through the cosmos with unprecedented speed. Such advancements may bring distant star systems within reach, thus broadening the scope of exploration and discovery.

As theories of hyperspace continue to evolve, the intersection with superstring theory propels humanity's aspirations beyond the terrestrial realm and into the cosmic fabric. This interplay raises profound questions about our understanding of existence, reality, and the complexities of the universe itself. Hyperspace travel not only invites us to contemplate the mechanics of movement across the stars but also challenges the boundaries of what defines our universe.

However, the journey into hyperspace and the implications of superstring theory are fraught with complexities and uncertainties. Theoretical challenges abound, particularly regarding how to practically manipulate higher dimensions and harness the energies required for such endeavors. Exotic matter, as mentioned previously, becomes crucial in stabilizing theoretical constructs like wormholes and warp drives, yet its existence remains unproven within established physics.

Moreover, the ethical considerations surrounding hyperspace travel resonate deeply within the broader narrative of interstellar exploration. As we strive to expand our reach among the stars, we must grapple with the potential consequences of accessing other dimensions, along with the responsibilities inherent in our pursuits. Questions arise about the implications of interacting with other celestial phenomena—some of which could be profoundly different from our own—including the impacts on extraterrestrial life forms and ecosystems.

In summary, the exploration of hyperspace and superstring theory offers a fertile ground for imagining the future of intergalactic travel. By delving into the complex interplay between dimensions, fundamental particles, and the very fabric of reality, we augment our understanding of space-time. While the theoretical discussions are rich with possibility, they also serve a more profound purpose: to illuminate our ambitions to explore the cosmos while grounding those aspirations in the ethical considerations that arise as we do so. As we remain on the frontier of cosmic inquiry, the revelations of hyperspace may indeed redefine our journey among the stars, positioning us closer to achieving the dream of intergalactic travel.

4.2. Dark Matter as a Conduit

The idea of dark matter as a conduit for intergalactic travel opens an intriguing avenue in both astrophysics and speculative scientific concepts surrounding stargates and cosmic highways. Dark matter, which comprises about 27% of the universe's total mass-energy content, remains largely enigmatic due to its non-luminous nature; it does not emit, absorb, or reflect light, making it invisible and detectable primarily through its gravitational effects. Although still not fully understood, the properties of dark matter may suggest pathways that could facilitate movement across vast cosmic distances —essentially acting as conduits that connect distant regions of space.

The gravitational influence of dark matter was first hypothesized to explain discrepancies between the observed rotational speeds of galaxies and the predicted values based on visible matter alone. This observation led to the realization that substantial masses must exist beyond our observational capabilities. It is hypothesized that dark matter forms a scaffolding of halos around galaxies, providing the necessary gravitational clout to hold them together and influencing their movements. But what if we could harness these gravitational forces? If dark matter could be manipulated or interacted with in specific ways, it might become a means to traverse interstellar distances swiftly and efficiently, effectively creating shortcuts through the fabric of space-time.

To conceptualize the role dark matter could play as a conduit, we must first examine the foundational principles of dark matter physics. Dark matter particles — potentially weakly interacting massive particles (WIMPs), axions, or other exotic candidates — might possess unique properties that could permit them to interact with matter and energy in ways we are yet to fully comprehend. If allying with existing theories surrounding wormholes or complex space-time dynamics, dark matter could theoretically facilitate the creation of stable portals within its gravitational network, effectively linking different regions across the cosmos.

Recent studies of gravitational waves and cosmic structure formation suggest that the distribution of dark matter affects the large-scale structure of the universe. This could pave the way for a deeper understanding of how to create traversable pathways, similar to constructing a highway amid varying terrains. A starship, positioned at the threshold of a dark matter concentration, might theoretically tap into these gravitational wells to facilitate a type of gravitational "slingshot," navigating unseen highways that connect galaxies. This idea bears resemblance to methods employed in physics to harness gravitational forces for space travel but expands it to a grander scale involving cosmic energy fields.

Additionally, the possible interaction between dark matter and exotic matter presents another fascinating angle. If dark matter can be utilized to stabilize a wormhole, perhaps through delivery of specific dark matter particles, it could heighten the feasibility of interstellar travel through these theoretical constructs. The combination of dark matter dynamics with existing or forthcoming technologies might lead to innovative approaches, such as gravity assists or warp fields that operate on this framework, potentially laying the groundwork for stargates that could bypass the constraints of light-speed travel.

To explore the implications of dark matter as a conduit for stargate operation, we must also consider the role of advanced detection technologies. As our ability to observe and interact with dark matter continues to evolve, enhanced methodologies for deciphering its properties could elucidate mechanisms by which we might exploit its gravitational effects. For example, the advancement of detectors designed to identify dark matter interactions on a fundamental level may unearth potential processes through which energy can be harvested or manipulated to create stable pathways.

In conjunction with this exploration, practical concerns arise regarding the ethics and safety of utilizing dark matter pathways. As humanity advances towards this tantalizing frontier, ethical reflections must accompany technological advancement. Examining the consequences of interacting with dark matter—an entity we presently know little about—plunges us into profound discussions regarding responsibility in our scientific undertakings. Should dark matter conduits be harnessed, rigorous protocols and guidelines must be established to ensure that explorations do not inadvertently disrupt the cosmic balances that govern the universe.

In conclusion, contemplating dark matter as a conduit for stargates represents a unique intersection of theoretical physics and the ambition that fuels humanity's desire to explore the cosmos. By engaging with the nature and properties of dark matter, we not only foster curiosity but also encourage speculative inquiry regarding the future of intergalactic travel. While still nestled within the realm of theoretical possibility, the prospects of utilizing dark matter can ignite discourse surrounding technological ambitions, ethical considerations, and the potential paths that may one day link us across the cosmos. As we continue our quest to uncover the secrets the universe holds, the exploration of dark matter may well illuminate the way forward, transforming our dreams of interstellar travel into navigable realities.

4.3. Astrophysical Anomalies as Gateways

Astrophysical anomalies have long captivated human imagination, inviting scientists and dreamers alike to speculate on the mysteries that pervade our universe. These phenomena—ranging from pulsars and black holes to cosmic microwave background radiation—may offer unexpected insights into the mechanics of interstellar travel and, potentially, serve as gateways for traversing vast cosmic distances. In this exploration, we will delve into a variety of astrophysical anomalies and assess their potential roles in connecting disparate regions of the universe, fundamentally shaping our understanding of travel beyond our solar system.

Pulsars, for instance, are rapidly rotating neutron stars that emit beams of electromagnetic radiation, acting as cosmic lighthouses. Their predictable pulsation provides astronomers with invaluable tools for navigation across the cosmos. Their stability allows them to serve as cosmic markers, similar to how lighthouses help navigate the sea. In a hypothetical framework of stargates or sidereal subways, pulsars could serve as beacons guiding ships through intergalactic pathways. By utilizing pulsar timing as a form of celestial navigation, travelers could orient themselves within the cosmic expanse, ensuring safe passage through otherwise impenetrable darkness.

Black holes present another fascinating aspect of astrophysical anomalies, encapsulating immense gravitational forces that warp the fabric of space-time itself. While typically viewed as one-way portals from which nothing can escape, theoretical models suggest that certain types of black holes—specifically rotating black holes or Kerr black holes—might allow for the existence of wormholes that connect distant regions of space-time. By theorizing about the potential accessibility of such structures, we can speculate on the possibility of using black holes as gateways for interstellar travel. The idea posits that if one were to navigate the extreme forces surrounding a rotating black hole with precision and knowledge of its dynamics, it might be possible to enter a wormhole that would open into another part of the universe, effectively bypassing the light-years that normally separate celestial bodies.

In addition to pulsars and black holes, the intriguing phenomenon of cosmic strings—hypothetical topological defects in the fabric of space-time—has also captured scientific interest. These one-dimensional threads of energy are theorized to form in the early universe and could possess immense mass density. Their potential gravitational influence might allow space-time to stretch and twist, creating pathways for interstellar travel. If harnessed correctly, cosmic strings might act as nodes within a vast network facilitating transport across significant distances. This innovative approach invites both contemplation and experimentation, as it encourages scientists to consider the diverse ways astrophysical anomalies might be integrated into future theories of travel and exploration.

Other anomalies, such as gamma-ray bursts (GRBs)—the most energetic explosions observed in the universe—may paradoxically provide insights into travel. While GRBs signal destructive cataclysms, their immense energy output presents an opportunity for exploration. Gravitational waves produced by the merging of neutron stars—often heralded by GRBs—carry information about the events that spawned them. Advanced observational technologies capable of detecting such waves could lead to a better understanding of the conditions surrounding them and their potential implications for interstellar pathways. Exploring the spatial configurations that accompany these cosmic phenomena may allow humanity to develop new insights concerning natural structures or energy supports for stargate constructions.

Astrophysical anomalies also intersect with broader discussions about energy harnessing and utilization for travel. Natural cosmic phenomena—such as solar flares or magnetic fields of planets—could be examined for their potential energy resources. If we could effectively capture and manipulate energies emitted during these events, it might lead to breakthroughs regarding propulsion systems, stargate maintenance, or even interstellar conduits. This reflects a fundamental tenet of exploration: the more we understand the universe's unpredictable behaviors, the better we can innovate technologies that facilitate reach across its domains.

The collective study of these astrophysical anomalies builds a framework that shifts our thinking from limitations to possibilities. By recognizing that certain phenomena may offer connective pathways between regions of space, we can theorize about constructing transit systems informed by cosmic reality. For instance, creating artificial constructs that leverage the gravitational effects of pulsars or black holes may yield novel technologies capable of facilitating travel and exploration beyond our own solar system.

However, as we delve into these ideas, ethical considerations surrounding space travel must remain central to our discourse. Navigating anomalies may pose potential risks to both travelers and to the cosmic environment. Therefore, exploring the implications of using such phenomena as gateways invites discussions on preserving universal balances, ensuring that humanity's reach does not inadvertently disrupt delicate ecosystems or intricate gravitational dynamics.

In conclusion, investigating astrophysical anomalies as gateways for interstellar travel illuminates profound avenues for exploration. By examining the characteristics of pulsars, black holes, cosmic strings, and other stellar phenomena, we can gain insight into possible structures and technologies that might facilitate cosmic journeys. The synthesis of astrophysical knowledge with technological innovation allows for a vision of the future where travel among the stars becomes a legitimate ambition, grounded in understanding. As we continue to explore these anomalies, we set the stage for possibilities that stretch beyond our imagination, hinting at the interconnectedness of the cosmos and our role within it.

4.4. Communicating Across the Cosmos

As we peer into the vast tapestry of the cosmos, the possibility of communicating across intergalactic distances presents both exhilarating opportunities and formidable challenges. The very act of maintaining coherent communication over such immense stretches of space stirs questions that intersect with advanced physics, technology, philosophy, and the very essence of what it means to connect as conscious beings in an ever-expanding universe.

At the most fundamental level, communication occurs through the transmission of signals, typically in the form of electromagnetic waves, which propagate through space as light does. However, when considering the staggering distances involved in intergalactic travel —distances measured in millions or even billions of light-years—the feasibility of transmitting signals becomes less straightforward. For instance, when we send a message to a distant star, we must account for the time it takes for that signal to travel at the speed of light. A signal sent to even the closest star systems can take several years to reach its destination, creating potential delays in communication that escalate dramatically with intergalactic distances.

The challenges of such latent communication are compounded when one considers the current technological limitations we face. Presently, our ability to send signals efficiently falters against the vastness of space; even with the most powerful radio telescopes and broadcasting equipment, the strength of signals diminishes over distance, leading to concerns over signal loss and degradation. Thus, as we conceptualize the architecture of decentralized stargate systems or interconnected sidereal subways, the infrastructure necessary for reliable communication emerges as an urgent need—one that demands innovative solutions and rigorous theoretical foundations.

One possible approach to enhancing intergalactic communication lies in the development of more advanced forms of signal transmission. Recent advancements indicate that using laser technology to send coherent light-based signals could significantly improve our ability to transmit data over vast distances. Laser communication systems promise to provide higher data rates and greater signal clarity, allowing for more intricate exchanges between interstellar probes and Earth. Coupled with powerful receivers capable of detecting faint signals, such technology could render the barriers of distance less daunting.

Moreover, the notion of utilizing quantum entanglement as a communication medium brings forth a fascinating avenue ripe for exploration. Quantum entanglement, the phenomenon where pairs of particles become correlated regardless of distance, suggests that changes to one particle instantaneously affect its partner—prompting speculation on the existence of "quantum communication." While this idea remains largely theoretical and faces practical challenges in its application, the prospect of instantaneous communication transcending light speed could redefine our communication paradigms in the cosmos.

Additionally, addressing the philosophy of communication across the universe compels us to contemplate the implications of conveying ideas, emotions, and consciousness through interstellar channels. If we were to communicate with intelligent extraterrestrial civilizations on distant planets—beings whose cultures, languages, and modes of thought differ drastically from our own—the transmission of information could become a rich yet complex endeavor. Efforts to establish a common language, symbols, or frameworks for understanding could pave a pathway toward mutual comprehension, giving rise to a dialogue between worlds.

However, the ethical considerations concerning communication also require nuanced reflection. As humanity embarks on its potential endeavors across the stars, the notion of seeding messages or signals into the universe prompts inquiries about the ramifications of reaching out. Will our attempts to communicate be met with curiosity, hostility, or indifference? Encouraging peaceful exchanges, defined by mutual respect and understanding, underlines the need for ethical guidance in our cosmic communications.

Finally, amidst the myriad challenges, the significance of building and lacing a cosmic communication network must be recognized. Such a network would not only serve as a channel between distant worlds but would also function as a means of sharing knowledge and cultures in a shared quest for understanding the universe's mysteries. As we move forward into the future, the possibilities of intergalactic communication ignite our imaginations, reinvigorating our commitment to forge connections that transcend the limitations of our existence on Earth.

As scholars, scientists, and dreamers work tirelessly to devise solutions for traversing the immense distances that separate us, the endeavor of communicating across the cosmos reflects our innate desire to understand and connect with the universe and other sentient beings therein. With each step we take toward mastering the intricacies of cosmic communication, we inch closer to a future where the wonders of the universe become accessible to our shared consciousness—a tapestry woven from the threads of inquiry, connection, and discovery.

4.5. Navigating the Sidereal Subway Systems

Navigating the Sidereal Subway Systems involves a comprehensive understanding of both the theoretical framework and practical techniques of intergalactic navigation in a universe filled with intricate connections and expansive distances. As we venture into the realm of sidereal subways—our metaphorical representation of advanced transit systems through space—we must articulate the landscape of potential navigation systems that would guide travelers across these celestial highways and scaffolds. The concept of sidereal subways evokes images of comprehensive networks that harness both the fabric of space-time and the perturbations within it, allowing for efficient travel between distant star systems.

At the core of navigating the sidereal subway systems is the development of detailed star maps that incorporate not only spatial coordinates but also comprehensive data related to cosmic phenomena, gravitational fields, and the presence of dark matter. Such maps would function as essential navigational tools, providing incredible detail about the various nodes within the intergalactic networks. By utilizing a combination of observational data and advanced predictive algorithms, navigators could chart courses through stable passages while avoiding regions where gravitational distortions or other anomalies might present hazards.

To further refine techniques in navigation, quantum computing technology could be harnessed to process vast amounts of data in real-time, ensuring that every traveler remains informed of their position within the sidereal subway system. Opting for quantum-assisted navigational systems, ships could calculate the optimal trajectories in an instant, accounting for gravitational influences from nearby celestial bodies, potential hazards, and even variances in the fabric of space-time. Such an approach not only enhances navigational accuracy but also paves the way for adaptive algorithms capable of responding to dynamic cosmic conditions.

In addition to conventional celestial navigation, leveraging the phenomena of gravitational lensing presents a unique opportunity for travelers navigating the sidereal subway system. Gravitational lensing—the bending of light caused by massive objects—can be utilized as natural markers that guide travelers along their routes. By mapping the lensing effects produced by galaxies, clusters, or dark matter concentrations, navigators could identify the most efficient pathways through the cosmic expanse. Understanding the interplay between the stars and their surrounding gravitational fields creates an intricate web of light that could be used to design multi-dimensional navigation systems.

Moreover, the role of artificial intelligence (AI) and machine learning becomes imperative in the context of navigating sidereal subway systems. AI could serve not merely as a pilot but as an autonomous navigator, assessing a ship's position, trajectory, and the plethora of variables at play within the navigation context. Such systems would utilize real-time data from both local systems and universal phenomena, ensuring that all potential threats and opportunities are considered during the journey. In this intricate dance of data and travel, AI could further enhance safety protocols, predict potential spatial obstacles, and implement course corrections instantaneously when unfamiliar patterns emerge in the surrounding space.

Map-making for these sidelines of the universe extends beyond mere geography; it also incorporates time. Factors such as time dilation —caused by the effects of gravity and speed on the passage of time —would demand nuanced calculations. For instance, if a ship travels close to a gravitational field or at relativistic speeds, navigators will need to adjust their perception of time on board versus that of their destination. This intersection of navigation and time perception poses intriguing challenges, requiring an integrated model of space-time that interrelates the twin dimensions as navigational aids.

As we probe deeper into the mechanics of navigating the sidereal subway systems, it is essential to consider the potential role of cosmic energies in navigation. Streamlining navigation would require tapping into the energies that permeate the universe, such as cosmic background radiation or harnessing solar wind patterns. By utilizing advanced sensors and energy conversion technologies, we could develop systems capable of continually gathering information about the environment, thereby enriching the navigational datasets that inform our journeys.

In conclusion, navigating the sidereal subway systems signifies an ambitious blend of human ingenuity, advanced technology, and theoretical physics. The essence of these intergalactic transport frameworks relies on developing sophisticated star maps, leveraging gravitational phenomena, and employing artificial intelligence to enhance the stability and reliability of travel routes. As we continue to refine our methods of navigation, we draw closer to the realization of a future where traveling among the stars melds seamlessly with the aspects of the universe that shape our journey. The possibilities are vast, urging us to explore and engage with the cosmic networks that await, connecting points in space and time with unfathomable potential.

5. Building Bridges to the Stars: Technological Feasibility

5.1. Current Technology and Its Constraints

As we venture into the realm of current technology and its inherent limitations, it is essential to examine the myriad of constraints that face us in our quest for intergalactic travel and the realization of concepts like stargates and sidereal subways. While the very notion of traversing cosmic distances may awaken a sense of possibility, the reality we confront today is steeped in technical, financial, and theoretical barriers that render such ambitions daunting.

At the core of these constraints lies our understanding of the laws of physics as currently established. The speed of light, an immutable constant in the universe as articulated by Einstein's theories of relativity, presents a formidable barrier to travel. It imposes limits on how quickly we can traverse the vast expanses of space. The vast interstellar and intergalactic distances mean that even within our solar neighborhood, reaching the nearest stars would take several years, if not decades, traveling at current technological speeds. Conventional spacecraft propulsion systems—reliant on chemical reactions or low-thrust electric propulsion—are insufficient for reaching speeds anywhere close to light speed.

Moreover, the propulsion systems we have today carry their own set of limitations. Current rocket technology, while an incredible achievement, is heavily reliant on chemical fuels and is not designed for prolonged travel or for the energy requirements needed to breach cosmic distances. The thrust-to-weight ratios of existing systems make them inefficient for interstellar missions. Development in advanced propulsion systems, such as nuclear thermal propulsion, ion drives, or theoretical concepts like antimatter or solar sails, might offer partial solutions; yet, even these remain speculative and face significant technical hurdles before they could be deemed practical for extended space travel.

Another crucial aspect of current technological constraints involves energy generation and management. Enabling a spacecraft capable of stargate operations necessitates extraordinary energy outputs—far beyond the capabilities of our existing power systems. Theoretical constructs like wormholes or warp drives posit that vast amounts of energy would be required to create the conditions for stable travel through exotic dimensions. Yet harnessing such energies poses intrinsic challenges. Conventional energy sources on Earth—fossil fuels, solar energy, or nuclear power—are inadequate when scaled to the levels needed for intergalactic travel. Research into harnessing fusion energy or tapping into cosmic phenomena, such as the energy of neutron stars or black holes, remains in nascent stages and serves to emphasize our reliance on yet-to-be-validated theories.

Furthermore, the environmental concerns tied to our current technology cannot be overlooked. The production of spacecraft involves significant material consumption, the extraction of rare resources, and the generation of waste—all of which contribute to the broader ecological footprint of space exploration activities. As humanity contemplates stretching beyond our planet, we must ensure that our technological advancements do not exacerbate existing environmental crises faced by Earth, particularly at a time when such challenges profoundly affect our sustainability.

Additionally, current information and navigational technologies pose constraints on our capability to explore and map the universe adequately. As we consider the grand scale of intergalactic travel, the limitations inherent in our observational technologies hinder our ability to gather comprehensive data about target star systems, their environments, potential hazards, and the cosmic phenomena that could facilitate interstellar journeys. The refinement of these technologies—highly sensitive telescopes, advanced sensors, and data analytical tools—is fundamental if we wish to navigate effectively through the complexities of the cosmos.

It is also imperative to acknowledge the socio-political constraints that tether the development of advanced spacefaring technologies.

The multifaceted interplay between science, funding, and international collaboration presents significant hurdles. Space exploration, and intergalactic travel in particular, hinges on substantial financial investments that are often subject to shifting political landscapes and competing national interests. While space agencies and private companies exhibit remarkable advancements, the scaling up of these efforts to achieve interstellar travel remains contingent upon collaborative investments and resources unlikely to materialize in the immediate future.

Finally, as we delve further into the intersection of technology and practicality, ethical implications emerge as formidable constraints within the conversation about stargates and sidereal subways. The prospect of intergalactic travel raises questions concerning the responsibilities we bear as humanity moves into the cosmos. The need to establish ethical frameworks surrounding exploration, resource extraction, and interactions with potential extraterrestrial ecosystems is essential if we are to navigate the ethical dilemmas and unforeseen consequences that our technological pursuits may unleash in the universe.

While the constraints of current technology present immense challenges to the prospects of intergalactic travel, they simultaneously serve to invigorate and direct inquiry into potential solutions. As we engage with these limitations critically, striving for advanced technologies that may one day enable us to traverse the cosmos, we cultivate a landscape ripe for discovery, innovation, and perseverance. The conversation surrounding stargates and sidereal subways acts not only as a reflection of human ambition but also as an acknowledgment of the substantial work that lies ahead, ensuring that we remain dedicated to overcoming the barriers conceiving the interstellar journeys of tomorrow. In navigating this complex landscape, we are challenged to forge effective paths toward an aspirational future, one that embodies the spirit of exploration while safeguarding our responsibilities to both our home planet and beyond.

5.2. Future Technologies on the Horizon

As we look to the future, the concept of stargate travel—once confined to the realm of science fiction—could become a plausible reality through a series of technological innovations and discoveries that are currently on the horizon. These advancements are not merely speculative; they represent the culmination of years of diligent research, interdisciplinary inquiry, and a burgeoning understanding of the universe's complexities. This exploration examines potential breakthroughs that may redefine our possibilities for traversing the cosmos.

One of the foremost innovations likely to influence intergalactic travel is the development of advanced propulsion systems. Traditional chemical propulsion methods, which we rely on today, are fundamentally limited by their energy efficiency and speed constraints. However, burgeoning research into alternative propulsion methodologies, such as nuclear thermal propulsion and plasma propulsion, holds promise for significantly enhancing spacecraft capabilities. Nuclear thermal propulsion, for instance, uses nuclear reactions to heat a propellant, promising a much higher specific impulse compared to conventional rocket engines. This advancement might allow spacecraft to accelerate more quickly and reach distant destinations faster, narrowing the time frames associated with interstellar travel.

Among the most tantalizing prospects for the future of stargate technology may lie in the realm of antimatter propulsion. Antimatter, the most exotic form of matter known to science, has the potential to yield energy releases orders of magnitude higher than conventional fuels. Harnessing the energy of antimatter could provide a feasible means for achieving relativistic speeds, perhaps making it possible to traverse vast distances in shorter time frames. Ongoing research is focusing on the production and containment of antimatter, laying the groundwork for this revolutionary form of propulsion.

Inextricably linked to the success of stargate technology is the quest for exotic matter—hypothetical materials predicted to have negative energy density. Consequently, the perception and manipulation of matter at this exotic level may be the key to creating stable traversable wormholes or warping space-time itself. Innovations in material science and high-energy physics are enabling researchers to explore the fundamental properties of matter in unprecedented ways, propelling the investigation into how materials may behave under extreme conditions. Advances in nanotechnology may further allow scientists to engineer materials with extraordinary properties, suggesting that we could one day create viable constructs to support the infrastructure necessary for stargate operation.

The integration of artificial intelligence (AI) and machine learning technologies also holds transformative potential for the future of travel through stargates. As the complexity of navigation systems associated with intergalactic journeys increases, AI can manage and analyze colossal datasets, optimize routes, and predict potential hazards in real time. Moreover, autonomous spacecraft equipped with AI can make decisions instantaneously based on current data, enhancing safety and efficiency in travel. Future advancements in AI will enable us to design more sophisticated interstellar spacecraft, equipped with intelligent systems that adapt to ever-changing cosmic environments.

Another critical area of exploration is our understanding of quantum physics, particularly phenomena such as quantum entanglement. Some researchers are postulating that quantum states could facilitate instantaneous communication over vast distances, possibly allowing for real-time coordination between travelers. This advancement may accompany the development of stargates, enabling efficient communication and navigation across the cosmos.

As we contemplate elements of infrastructure that may support intergalactic travel, the integration of advanced energy harvesting techniques appears paramount. Innovative methods of harnessing cosmic energies—be it from solar flares, cosmic radiation, or even the rotational energy of celestial bodies—could provide the necessary power for stargate operations. For instance, concepts related to Dyson spheres—massive structures designed to capture energy from stars

—could evolve to encompass methods for harvesting energy from a variety of celestial processes.

Intergalactic explorations will likely push the boundaries of our understanding of the physical universe. As we discover and create technologies that might allow stargates to function, we may also find new phenomena, unexpected cosmic structures, or peculiar laws governing the behaviors of matter. Just as with the revelations accompanying developments in relativity and quantum mechanics, these discoveries will reshape our understanding of reality itself.

In conclusion, the future of intergalactic travel through stargates hinges on a spectrum of transformative technologies poised to revolutionize our approach to traversing the cosmos. From advanced propulsion systems and exotic matter manipulation to harnessing cosmic energies and integrating artificial intelligence, the road ahead is paved with possibilities. As we stand on the cusp of a new era of exploration and understanding, the innovations on the horizon challenge us to expand our visions and rethink our relationship to the universe. The dream of stargate travel may no longer be a distant fantasy but one step closer to becoming a tangible reality, inviting us to embrace our destiny among the stars.

5.3. Infrastructure of the Unseen

The theoretical framework for intergalactic transit systems—encompassing stargates, sidereal subways, and other potential constructs —relies on a robust infrastructure of unseen materials and mechanisms that must transcend our current technological and scientific limitations. As we delve into the nuances of this infrastructure, several essential components become apparent, each holding the key to unlocking the mysteries of intergalactic travel and ensuring safe navigation through the cosmos.

One of the foundational elements of this infrastructure lies in the conceptualization of exotic matter, a theoretical substance that possesses negative mass and energy density. Exotic matter is postulated to play a crucial role in stabilizing traversable wormholes created within the space-time continuum, enabling the creation of stable pathways between distant points in the universe. To navigate the implications of intergalactic travel, we must first understand the properties of this matter and the conditions under which it can be generated or manipulated. Research into high-energy particle physics may unearth new particles or conditions conducive to the existence of exotic matter, offering new pathways to explore its potential applications in stargate technology.

Additionally, the materials required for the construction of stargates and sidereal subway systems must be immensely durable and capable of withstanding the extreme conditions inherent in the cosmos. Advanced materials science will play a pivotal role in identifying such materials, focusing on those that exhibit exceptional strength, flexibility, and stability. For example, materials engineered at the molecular level, such as graphene and carbon nanotubes, display properties that could lend themselves to the creation of structures capable of harnessing the gravitational forces associated with black holes or the fluctuating energies present in wormholes.

The architectural designs of stargates themselves must also be addressed within the infrastructure of the unseen. The theoretical blueprints for such constructs demand multilevel systems capable of managing the immense gravitational, thermal, and kinetic stresses incurred during operation. Diagrams and simulations could help ascertain the geometric configurations best suited for maintaining stability across potentially chaotic environments. Computational models simulating the behaviors of these structures amidst gravitational perturbations and temporal distortions will be instrumental in determining how to build and maintain stargates efficiently.

Furthermore, the infrastructure would encompass energy-harvesting technologies essential for sustaining stargate operation. This burden could be shared between advanced solar sails that capture solar energy from nearby stars and energy-conversion systems capable of tapping into the gravitational pull of massive cosmic bodies. Innovations in energy storage and transfer technologies will be paramount in ensuring that harvested energy can be effectively and efficiently redirected to power the stargate infrastructure. The integration of artificial intelligence (AI) for managing energy flows, predictive analytics, and real-time adjustments will enhance our ability to efficiently utilize cosmic energies to maintain the operational integrity of the system.

Moreover, the necessity of communication infrastructure cannot be overstated, as reliable communication is crucial for not only navigating sidereal subway systems but also coordinating between an array of starships, ground stations, and control centers. Advanced quantum communication technologies could forge instantaneous connections across vast distances, allowing for seamless information exchange amidst the complexities of interstellar transit. Such innovations involve harnessing quantum entanglement principles, enabling the rapid transfer of information independent of space-time constraints and fostering collaborative efforts across distant explorations.

As we ponder the intricacies of infrastructure, it is essential to consider the interconnectivity of these unseen elements. The interplay between materials, energy systems, navigational technology, and communication networks creates a harmonious environment that fuels our aspirations for intergalactic travel. Speculating on how these diverse components could coalesce necessitates a forward-thinking approach to technological collaboration, embracing interdisciplinary research from theoretical physics to advanced engineering.

Ultimately, envisioning the infrastructure of the unseen serves as a metaphorical canvas upon which we paint the future of intergalactic travel. This mental image evokes a world where humanity harnesses the vast potential of the cosmos, engaging in a cosmic conversation that transcends the boundaries of our earthly existence. As we continue to investigate, experiment, and innovate, the dream of constructing stargates and sidereal subways inches closer to tangible realization, promising an extraordinary journey among the stars awaits. The task ahead will require not only scientific ingenuity but also an enduring ethical commitment to navigating the complexities of our cosmic ambitions with wisdom, care, and respect for the fabric of the universe we seek to explore.

5.4. Harnessing Cosmic Energies

Harnessing cosmic energies for intergalactic travel represents a pivotal leap in our understanding of both physics and technology. The intricate dance of celestial bodies and the cosmic phenomena that surround them offers a treasure trove of potential energy sources, each with its own unique applications and implications for future travel beyond our solar system. As we explore the various mechanisms through which we might capture and utilize these energies, we confront both opportunities for innovation and ethical considerations inherent in our quest for the stars.

One of the most promising avenues for harnessing cosmic energies lies in the activity of stars themselves. Solar energy harvesting has long been a topic within the realm of energy generation on Earth, but its potential in space is exponentially greater. Space-based solar panels positioned at optimal alignments could tap into the unfiltered energy of our Sun, as well as capturing solar winds—streams of charged particles emanating from the solar corona. Utilizing robust and flexible photovoltaic materials or advanced solar sails could allow for the collection of vast quantities of energy, subsequently converted into usable power for spacecraft propulsion or the operation of stargates.

In the context of intergalactic travel, solar energy becomes particularly significant due to its abundance throughout the universe. By establishing infrastructure such as solar farms around stars, we could create vast networks capable of transmitting harvested energy across great distances. The energy collected could be beamed laser-like or harnessed using directed energy systems back to receiving stations, including spacecraft or stargate networks, thus ensuring a sustainable and renewable energy supply for transit far beyond our solar confines.

Another celestial source of power comes from the rotational energy of massive astronomical bodies, such as pulsars or neutron stars. These spinning remnants of supernovae release immense amounts of energy, producing gravitational waves and radiation patterns that could potentially be captured. For example, the hypothetical concept of a Dyson sphere—a mega-structure designed to encompass a star and capture its output—could be adapted to harness the energy emitted by a pulsar or neutron star. Such structures would enable the extraction of tremendous amounts of rotational energy over extended periods, offering an impressive reservoir for future deep-space expeditions.

Additionally, cosmic rays may offer another avenue for exploration in harnessing energy. Cosmic rays, highly energetic particles originating from distant astrophysical processes, bombard the Earth and travel through the cosmos at light speed. Researchers are investigating advanced techniques for utilizing these high-energy particles as catalysts for energy generation or propulsion. Conceptual frameworks for energy conversion could allow us to effectively redirect and harness cosmic ray energy, potentially enabling spacecraft to fuel their journeys through intergalactic space without relying solely on chemical or nuclear power.

Furthermore, black holes—often cast in a mysterious light—may serve as an unprecedented source of energy. The process of Hawking radiation, proposed by physicist Stephen Hawking, hypothesizes that black holes emit radiation due to quantum effects near their event horizons. Capturing the energy released during matter accretion or the hypothetical emissions of Hawking radiation poses a tantalizing challenge for future energy technologies. By developing methods to safely extract and utilize energy from black holes, humanity could facilitate significant advancements in propulsion technology, potentially opening gateways for rapid interstellar travel.

The exploration of potential energy sources doesn't stop with celestial phenomena; advances in technologies such as fusion energy also present exciting prospects. Harnessing fusion, the process that powers stars, could yield near-limitless energy outputs without the harmful byproducts associated with fossil fuels. Fusion reactors operating on the principles of high-temperature plasma containment might one day be developed for use in spacecraft or stargates, permitting sustained energy required for operating intergalactic transit systems.

As we envisage harnessing these cosmic energies, it is critical to consider the infrastructure necessary for their collection, conversion, and transmission. This infrastructure would need to be resilient enough to withstand the adverse conditions of space while being flexible enough to adapt to the variety of energy inputs. The complexities of engineering such systems and ensuring they can operate reliably across varying cosmic environments remain monumental challenges to be addressed.

Moreover, the ethical considerations surrounding energy harvesting must not be overlooked. As we aspire to draw from the cosmos, we must cultivate a sense of custodianship regarding how we interact with celestial environments. The act of harnessing energy poses questions about the long-term implications of our activities on the overall balance of cosmic ecosystems. Thus, developing guidelines to ensure sustainable practices in energy collection will be essential in guiding our endeavors.

In conclusion, the harnessing of cosmic energies illuminates promising pathways toward intergalactic travel. By tapping into the abundant resources offered by celestial phenomena, including solar energy, gravitational forces, pulsars, cosmic rays, and even black holes, we may pave the way for advanced propulsion systems that make traversing the distances between stars a tangible reality. Each step forward in capturing and using these energies instills a sense of hope and wonder, inviting us to imagine a future where humanity ventures beyond its home planet to explore the vast expanse of the cosmos. As we prepare for these grand adventures, we must remain vigilant in our commitment to ethical practices, ensuring that our cosmic exploration enriches rather than disrupts the delicate balances that characterize the universe.

5.5. AI and Autonomous Systems in Space Travel

In the evolving realm of space exploration, the advent of artificial intelligence (AI) and autonomous systems represents a transformative leap forward, promising innovative solutions to the complex challenges associated with intergalactic travel and the navigation of sidereal subway systems. As we contemplate the mechanics of traversing the vast, uncharted reaches of space, AI serves as a vital cornerstone for enhancing the safety, efficiency, and effectiveness of future exploratory efforts. The integration of AI systems into spacecraft and navigation protocols can provide an unprecedented level of precision and adaptability, allowing humanity to forge pathways among the stars.

At its core, AI can enable autonomous spacecraft to operate effectively and efficiently beyond our home planet. By integrating advanced sensory arrays and decision-making algorithms, these intelligent systems can autonomously navigate through cosmic terrains while responding to real-time phenomena. For instance, during the journey across interstellar distances, autonomous systems equipped with AI can continuously analyze data from onboard sensors, assessing surroundings for potential hazards such as asteroid fields, cosmic dust, or gravitational anomalies. Such capabilities allow for rapid adjustments to the spacecraft's trajectory, enhancing the safety of the vessel and its occupants and reducing reliance on distant control centers on Earth.

Moreover, the incorporation of AI into interstellar travel mechanisms can enhance the efficacy of resource management aboard spacecraft. Given the likelihood of long-duration missions, AI can optimize energy consumption, cargo handling, and life-support systems to ensure sustainability throughout the journey. Machine learning algorithms can analyze existing data on energy consumption patterns, adjusting these systems in real-time to maximize efficiency while minimizing waste. This dynamic resource management will be crucial as travelers venture farther from home, where traditional supply lines are not available.

The realms of data processing and analysis also benefit immensely from AI integration. Space missions generate vast amounts of information from numerous scientific instruments and sensors. Autonomous systems can swiftly compile, filter, and interpret this data, identifying potential areas of interest for further study while reducing the need for constant oversight from ground control. This capacity for autonomous data processing enables scientists and researchers to focus their efforts on more significant challenges, fostering a culture of innovation within the exploratory community.

In the context of navigating sidereal subway systems and their potential stargates, AI can facilitate precise mapping and coordination of cosmic pathways. Advanced algorithms linked to stellar and gravitational mapping information could yield complex models representing effective transit corridors among various celestial bodies. Armed with this navigational intelligence, both autonomous and piloted spacecraft can engage effectively with the vast cosmic highways, optimizing routes and minimizing travel times while ensuring that navigational courses align with the current understanding of astrophysical phenomena.

Security and safety considerations remain paramount in intergalactic travel, and AI can play a pivotal role in safeguarding missions against evolving threats. By incorporating machine learning, systems can be trained to recognize anomalies and potential risks, alerting crew members or executing predefined safety protocols proactively. During journeys through unpredictable cosmic terrains, on-the-fly analysis may be essential for identifying changes in environmental conditions and adapting navigation paths accordingly.

Autonomous AI systems also lend themselves to conducting preliminary investigations on celestial bodies—an important aspect of the exploration process that may precede human visits. By deploying robots or drones equipped with AI, we can collect geological samples, examine atmospheric conditions, and assess potential suitability for human habitation. These preliminary assessments not only minimize risks to human life but also inform decision-making concerning future missions, paving the way for sustainable exploration and potential colonization efforts.

However, as we embrace the capabilities of AI in space exploration, it is crucial to consider the ethical dimensions associated with integrating these systems into interstellar travel. The increased autonomy of AI raises questions about accountability, decision-making, and the nature of human oversight. As autonomous systems take on more responsibilities, we must grapple with who bears the responsibility for their actions—be it scientists, engineers, or the AI themselves. Establishing clear ethical frameworks will be vital for guiding the development of AI technologies and ensuring that missions respect both human values and the integrity of potential extraterrestrial ecosystems.

In conclusion, the integration of artificial intelligence and autonomous systems into space travel heralds a new era of exploration, characterized by increased safety, efficiency, and adaptability in navigating the cosmos. As humanity embarks on journeys to distant galaxies through stargates and sidereal subway systems, AI will serve as an invaluable ally—empowering travelers with the tools needed to face the challenges posed by the vast unknown. Amid the excitement of intergalactic travel, we must remain vigilant in addressing the ethical implications surrounding these advancements, ensuring that our quest for knowledge remains rooted in responsible stewardship and respect for the universe we seek to explore. As we build the future of space exploration, fostering a symbiotic relationship between humanity and technology will empower us to reach new heights and unlock the mysteries of the cosmos.

6. Safeguards and Ethics of Intergalactic Travel

6.1. Moral and Ethical Considerations

As humanity navigates the uncharted waters of interstellar travel, we must confront a myriad of moral and ethical considerations that arise within this ambitious frontier. The potential to explore, inhabit, or even terraform other worlds evokes not just excitement and wonder but also deep ethical scrutiny concerning our responsibilities toward these celestial bodies, their discovery, and the beings that may inhabit them—or may come to share our path.

Central to these ethical concerns is the principle of stewardship. As we embark on journeys to other worlds, the question emerges: What inherent rights do those worlds possess, and how do we respect them? The temptation to exploit extraterrestrial resources may rise, especially for a civilization observing rapid population growth and resource depletion on Earth. However, exploiting these environments for earthly desires must be counterbalanced by our commitment to being responsible custodians of the universe. We must seriously consider whether we have the authority to make decisions that could irrevocably alter an ecosystem we have yet to fully understand. This necessitates a cautious, well-researched approach grounded in ethical frameworks that emphasize respect for all forms of life and the ecosystems that support them, mirroring the principles of conservation we strive to uphold on our home planet.

Furthermore, the question of potential colonization raises pressing moral dilemmas. If we encounter intelligent extraterrestrial life forms, it is vital to address the ethical considerations tied to our interactions with them. History offers numerous examples from Earth of how encounters between advanced civilizations and those deemed 'lesser' culminated in exploitation, oppression, or destruction. These historical lessons serve as strong reminders to approach any engagement with extraterrestrial beings with respect, humility, and the recognition of their intrinsic rights as sentient entities. Treating alien species as equal partners in interstellar exploration could foster cooperation rather than conflict, presenting opportunities for shared growth rather than a continuation of humanity's historical patterns of dominance.

The ethical implications also extend to the socio-cultural fabric of Earth itself. Intergalactic travel may significantly alter cultural identities, paradigms, and traditional practices, leading to transformative effects that can resonate far beyond the act of exploration. The integration of new forms of knowledge accrued from interactions with extraterrestrial civilizations could challenge established beliefs and practices. While this presents an invaluable chance for evolution and growth, it also poses the risk of cultural homogenization. As we confront the possibilities of cross-cultural exchanges, it is crucial to uphold respect for diversity and maintain the richness of Earth's myriad cultures. Encouraging dialogues that bridge gaps between civilizations can illuminate paths forward that celebrate diversity rather than diminishment.

Legal frameworks governing cosmic exploration must also be established to aid in navigating these ethical currents. As governments and private entities begin pursuing interstellar ventures, the absence of established guidelines raises concerns regarding ownership, exploitation, and accountability. Establishing international policies will create structures that preside over cosmic activities, providing frameworks that prioritize peaceful exploration and equitable sharing of benefits. Such frameworks can help foster collaborations that are grounded in mutual respect, ensuring that no single entity possesses unilateral control over entire celestial bodies—a concern mirrored in the ongoing discussions surrounding ownership of Earth's resources.

In addition, we must consider the potential risks associated with traveling to and colonizing other worlds. What unforeseen consequences may arise from introducing Earth life forms into alien ecosystems? The risks of cross-contamination warrant extensive consideration, both for the ecosystems into which we might integrate and our own species as we navigate the unfamiliar biological landscapes of extraterrestrial environments. An ethical responsibility emerges to safeguard the integrity of both new worlds and our biological heritage.

Throughout these discussions, there remains an intrinsic link between knowledge, discovery, and ethical duties. The pursuit of knowledge through interstellar travel is a shared endeavor that requires collaborative engagement, thoughtful discourse, and ethical deliberation. By grounding our explorations in principles that honor diverse ecosystems, respect sentient life, and celebrate the richness of Earth's cultures, we advance our quest for knowledge and experience in a manner that emphasizes responsibility, humility, and an enduring commitment to the cosmos.

As we expand our horizons and contemplate future interactions beyond the stars, the ethical frameworks we establish today may serve as a testament to our character as a species—one that seeks not merely to conquer or exploit but rather to connect, learn, and coexist, ultimately transforming the dreams of intergalactic travel into a journey that uplifts and engages all life forms in a shared commitment to stewardship and exploration. In this light, the moral and ethical considerations woven into the fabric of interstellar travel call for a broader consciousness that reflects our aspirations for a just and equitable universe.

6.2. Maintaining Biodiversity

The intricate relationship between biodiversity and the pursuit of intergalactic travel raises significant ethical and practical considerations essential for ensuring the sustainable exploration of potential new worlds beyond our own. As humanity stands on the precipice of interstellar exploration, it is crucial to recognize the essential role that biodiversity plays not only on Earth but as we contemplate future encounters in the cosmos. A comprehensive understanding of how to maintain biodiversity is foundational to the integrity of ecosystems both terrestrial and extraterrestrial.

Our planet's biodiversity encompasses the rich variety of life forms, ecological systems, and genetic diversity within species that contribute to the balance of ecosystems. Each species plays a unique role in its habitat, influencing the functioning and resilience of ecological systems. As we embark on endeavors that may take us to distant planets or moons, we enter uncharted territories where existing ecosystems could be profoundly affected by our presence. The concepts of biodiversity preservation must become intrinsic to our approach to intergalactic travel, urging us to engage in practices that protect and manage life in all its forms.

To effectively maintain biodiversity amid interstellar exploration, we must first consider the ecological principles guiding the establishment of environmental stewardship. This begins with understanding the limits and potentials of Earth-based life forms when introduced into alien environments. While space agencies have researched ecological preservation protocols, the unknown variables in alien ecosystems necessitate a cautious approach that emphasizes research and adaptability. Rigorous ecological assessments should precede any introduction of Earth-origin species, enabling scientists to predict potential impacts and minimize risks of adverse interactions.

A promising avenue for maintaining biodiversity lies in utilizing advanced biotechnologies, such as bioengineering and synthetic biology. These technologies can be harnessed to create resilient life forms that are specifically designed for adaptation in varied extraterrestrial environments. By leveraging our growing understanding of genetic engineering, we can engineer organisms capable of thriving in extreme conditions, such as high radiation or low gravity, without disrupting their ecosystems. This approach emphasizes precision and foresight in the design of life forms, ultimately enabling the exploration of other worlds while minimizing ecological footprints.

Moreover, emerging practices in conservation biology can inform our interstellar aspirations. Preservation strategies aimed at habitat conservation, ecological restoration, and the establishment of protected areas can be adapted to interplanetary contexts. The philosophy of "no degradation" in the face of exploration or colonization should guide our ventures, preserving the integrity of any ecosystems we encounter. Establishing designated zones for ecological research and monitoring prior to any significant human intervention can provide invaluable insights into the functioning of extraterrestrial ecosystems, informing decisions that respect their inherent balances.

Adoption of principles from the precautionary approach can further support biodiversity maintenance. This approach advocates for proactive action to prevent harm to ecosystems even before definitive evidence of potential negative impacts exists. As we engage with untested ecosystems, exercising caution and humility permits us to avoid the historical pitfalls associated with colonial exploitation of lands and resources on Earth. By prioritizing biodiversity preservation explicitly, we encourage a mindset shift that values the interconnectedness of life—both on our home planet and beyond—cultivating an ethic of responsibility.

The challenges associated with maintaining biodiversity must also engage diplomatic considerations as interstellar travel unfolds. Collaborative frameworks among nations, space agencies, and potentially extraterrestrial civilizations must prioritize conservation efforts as humanity expands into the cosmos. International agreements establishing guiding principles for sustainable practices can facilitate effective ecological stewardship shared by all parties involved. Such dialogues embody a commitment to mutual respect for the rights of ecosystems and life forms, ensuring a cohesive approach to transiting between worlds.

Importantly, the educational dimensions of fostering biodiversity awareness accompany all explorative endeavors. Scientists, engineers, policy-makers, and the general public must embrace enlightened principles regarding the importance of biodiversity and its preservation. Knowledge-sharing and best practices surrounding biodiversity should become integral to the public discourse on intergalactic travel, providing avenues for collective action while fostering a more holistic understanding of the value of all living systems.

In summary, maintaining biodiversity in the face of intergalactic exploration necessitates a multi-dimensional approach that considers ecological, technological, ethical, and diplomatic factors. Acknowledging the interconnectedness of life forms and ecosystems—on Earth and beyond—serves as a foundational principle as we navigate the complexities of the cosmos. By prioritizing biodiversity preservation within the framework of our collective cosmic aspirations, we can shape an interstellar future that embodies not only the courage of exploration but the wisdom of stewardship. In doing so, we embrace a holistic view of our place in the universe that respects and cherishes the rich variegation of life—this pursuit extending beyond Earth, driving our evolution as compassionate stewards of existence across the stars.

6.3. The Risk of Cross-Contamination

The realm of intergalactic travel, while filled with promise and possibility, is fraught with risks, particularly the specter of cross-contamination between Earth organisms and potential extraterrestrial ecosystems. This risk extends beyond mere environmental concerns; it encompasses complex ethical, biological, and sociological implications that could have far-reaching consequences. As humanity prepares to engage with the cosmos on a deeper level, understanding and mitigating the risk of cross-contamination becomes imperative.

Cross-contamination refers to the unintended transfer of biological materials, such as microorganisms, plants, or animals, between distinct ecosystems. In the context of intergalactic travel, this could mean the introduction of Earth-origin life forms to alien environments—or vice versa—potentially destabilizing local ecosystems. The implications of such occurrences could range from minor ecological shifts to catastrophic collapses, depending on the nature of the interactions. For instance, Earth microbes, which have evolved alongside specific terrestrial environments, may thrive in alien ecosystems devoid of natural predators or competitors, leading to the outcompeting of native life forms and significant biodiversity loss.

The potential for cross-contamination raises crucial questions around the biosafety of space missions. As we explore new worlds, the introduction of Earth species could disrupt delicate environmental balances. Just as invasive species can wreak havoc on fragile habitats on our planet, the transference of Earth organisms to extraterrestrial settings may yield analogous outcomes. It is essential to implement stringent biosecurity measures when engaging in extraterrestrial exploration to prevent the transfer of terrestrial microbes or spores that could survive in space or on alien surfaces.

Robust planetary protection policies will be crucial as we embark on missions to explore celestial bodies, especially those believed to harbor life, such as Mars or specific moons of Jupiter and Saturn like Europa and Enceladus. These policies must encompass multiple strategies ranging from sterilization techniques for probes and landers to meticulous monitoring of contaminants aboard spacecraft. Technologies such as UV sterilization or chemical disinfectants could be employed during spacecraft assembly and before launch to mitigate risks.

Additionally, the concept of forward and backward contamination must also be addressed. Forward contamination refers to sending Earth organisms to other planetary bodies, while backward contamination involves bringing alien organisms back to Earth. Each scenario presents unique bioethical implications and technical challenges. For example, if a human crew returns from an exploratory mission with samples of extraterrestrial life, the potential implications for Earth's biosphere could be significant. These issues call for the development of comprehensive frameworks for assessing and managing the risks associated with sample return missions.

Ethically, the risk of cross-contamination evokes profound reflections on our responsibilities as explorers. The drive to discover and expand our knowledge must be tempered by the cognizance of the potential consequences our actions may have on alien worlds. Recognizing the intrinsic right of ecosystems to exist and thrive without undue influence from Earth life forms demands a deeper commitment to responsible exploration. Exploring new worlds should not equate to exploiting them. Instead, our approach must reflect an ethos of stewardship that safeguards the integrity of the ecosystems we engage with.

In light of these considerations, cross-contamination protocols and biosafety guidelines must be rooted in a collaborative, interdisciplinary framework. Biologists, astrobiologists, ethicists, engineers, and policymakers should unite to formulate comprehensive strategies addressing the myriad dimensions of cross-contamination risk. Global cooperation will become especially vital as nations and private entities embark on ambitious space exploration endeavors. Establishing international treaties and agreements could facilitate the sharing of best practices, ensuring that all parties prioritize biosafety in their cosmic activities.

As we navigate toward a future filled with exciting intergalactic travel possibilities, the risk of cross-contamination must be a defining factor in how we engage with the universe. The dual imperatives of scientific discovery and environmental stewardship should guide our actions as we journey through the cosmos. By prioritizing biosafety and responsible exploration, we endeavor not only to preserve the integrity of extraterrestrial ecosystems but also to uphold the ethical principles that underpin humanity's legacy as explorers of the stars.

The challenges posed by cross-contamination may prove to be daunting, yet they also inspire a sense of responsibility and aspiration. In our quest to unveil the mysteries of the universe, the pursuit of knowledge need not come at the expense of safeguarding the precious life forms and ecosystems that may exist beyond our own planet. Rather, our exploration should become an integrative journey marked by respect, curiosity, and reverence for all forms of life—a guiding light within the fabric of our ambitious cosmic endeavors. As we prepare to embrace our role as intergalactic explorers, it is essential that we do so with humility and care, echoing the commitment to a sustainable and ethical approach to our exploration of the unfolding tapestry of the universe.

6.4. Cultural Impacts on Earth and Beyond

The pursuit of intergalactic travel not only holds the promise of expanding humanity's reach beyond Earth's confines but also invokes profound cultural implications that ripple across our social structures. As we venture into this uncharted territory, we must acknowledge the substantial impact that interstellar exploration—through technologies such as stargates and sidereal subways—may have on our cultural paradigms, identity constructions, and the very fabric of human societies.

At the heart of the cultural impacts of intergalactic travel is the potential for a paradigm shift in how humanity perceives itself, its place in the cosmos, and its relationships with one another. Historically, human identity has been closely tied to our planetary existence, with cultures evolving in relation to geological, biological, and ecological contexts. The introduction of intergalactic travel propels us to reconsider these fundamental narratives. No longer merely Earth-centered beings, we may emerge as cosmic citizens linked to a vast universe, provoking reflections on our collective identity and aspirations.

This shift carries implications for art, literature, and language—domains inherently reflective of cultural dynamics. Works of art and storytelling that explore themes of space exploration, extraterrestrial encounters, and the search for meaning in the cosmos will flourish, shaping new narratives that invite audiences to reimagine their connections to both the universe and each other. The vastness of space may evoke questions about existence, awakening a new wave of philosophical exploration that traverses cultural boundaries. Literature and cinema will play pivotal roles in crafting narratives that not only entertain but also inspire dialogues across cultures regarding our shared responsibilities and aspirations as we chart paths among the stars.

Moreover, the presence of diverse cultures within humanity could influence approaches to interstellar exploration. As we venture beyond our boundaries, the values and beliefs of different civilizations must integrate into our explorative ethos, fostering collaboration and understanding. The principle of inclusivity will be paramount as we collectively engage with new worlds and explore the implications of life beyond Earth. The cultural heritages and philosophies of indigenous and marginalized groups should inform our cosmic pursuits, generating a rich tapestry of perspectives and fostering a sense of shared destiny.

Notably, the technological advancements behind intergalactic travel could also spur new cultural expressions. The advent of AI, robotics, and other transformative technologies may redefine human interactions, relationships, and even our conceptualizations of agency and personhood. The merging of human and machine, whether facilitated through autonomous systems or bioengineering, presents intricate cultural dynamics that challenge traditional boundaries. As societies adapt to these innovations, cultural expressions surrounding identity will evolve, reflecting both the potential of technology to enhance human experience and the ethical inquiry associated with these transformations.

In addition to the impacts on individual and collective identity, intergalactic travel may stimulate a reexamination of cultural and ethical frameworks. The potential discovery of extraterrestrial life forms would force humanity to confront fundamental questions about existence, consciousness, and the nature of life itself. This encounter could prompt widespread cultural and philosophical introspection, as well as debates regarding our responsibilities toward other sentient beings. Engaging thoughtfully with the values and ethics surrounding these encounters is critical for fostering an inclusive and respectful approach to new forms of life.

As we consider the prospects of intergalactic travel, we must also acknowledge the cultural ramifications of potential colonialism or exploitation. If encounters with alien civilizations occur, there is a risk that historical patterns of dominance, oppression, and exploitation may resurface. The lessons of our own colonial past should inform our collective consciousness as we strive for approaches that prioritize diplomacy, mutual benefit, and the preservation of cultural identities, both terrestrial and extraterrestrial. Building alliances founded on respect and empathy will be essential in navigating these uncharted waters.

Beyond the immediate impact on Earth's cultures, the dissemination of knowledge and technology through intergalactic exploration may foster a renewed sense of global cooperation. The endeavor to explore the cosmos may unite nations, transcending traditional divisions fueled by politics or ideologies. Reflecting on our shared humanity can inspire collaborative efforts aimed at solving pressing global challenges, such as climate change and resource depletion. As we become stewards of the stars, the potential to advocate for peace and unity will emerge as a powerful narrative, shaping cultural discourse and inspiring collective action.

In conclusion, the cultural impacts of intergalactic travel touch upon numerous facets of human existence—from identity constructions and artistic expressions to ethical reflections and global cooperation. The journey toward the stars calls us to cultivate a profound awareness of our interconnectedness and responsibility to one another and the universe. We stand at a precipice, poised to weave a dynamic narrative that embraces inclusivity, curiosity, and respect as we explore the vastness of the cosmos. Navigating this cultural landscape invites us to engage with the complexities of existence and contemplate the possibilities that await us amid the stars. Embracing diversity, empathy, and shared stewardship can pave the way for an exciting new chapter in the human story—one that enriches our cultural heritage as we journey among the galaxies.

6.5. Legal Frameworks for Cosmic Exploration

With the dawn of intergalactic travel, the imperative to establish robust legal frameworks governing cosmic exploration has never been more crucial. As humanity stands on the precipice of potentially transformative journeys into the cosmos, there exists a pressing need for collaborative international policies and agreements that can regulate and promote peaceful endeavors. These frameworks must address a spectrum of concerns, from resource utilization and environmental protection to the ethical treatment of potential extraterrestrial life-forms.

Historically, the foundations of space law emerged from the 1967 Outer Space Treaty, which marked a significant moment in international relations. This treaty established key principles, including the prohibition of the militarization of outer space, the commitment to peaceful exploration, and the stipulation that celestial bodies cannot be claimed by any single nation. However, as we contemplate intergalactic travel, the implications of these existing laws require reevaluation to accommodate the complexities and ethical considerations inherent in deeper exploration of the cosmos.

A primary facet to consider is the development of a framework governing the use of resources obtained from celestial bodies. As spacefaring technologies advance, the potential for resource extraction from asteroids, moons, and planets raises essential legal questions about ownership and stewardship. Current frameworks, which primarily focus on Earth and its resources, may not adequately address scenarios where mining operations or other resource utilization activities take place on celestial bodies. Thus, the establishment of an international treaty addressing resource governance—specifically concerning the use of extraterrestrial materials—holds paramount importance in ensuring fairness and preventing exploitation.

Another critical consideration revolves around the environmental implications of cosmic exploration. Just as environmental protections have become a cornerstone of terrestrial governance, so too must we extend these protections to the broader cosmos. Any activities that may impact the ecosystems of celestial bodies—be it through contamination, alteration, or introduction of Earth organisms—demand stringent regulatory oversight. Legal frameworks must emerge to mandate pre-emptive ecological assessments, combined with remediation obligations to address any inadvertent damage caused by exploratory activities. These frameworks can be modeled after international environmental agreements to ensure comprehensive protection of off-Earth ecosystems.

In the context of potential contact with extraterrestrial life, there exists an equally imperative need to define ethical guidelines that govern our interactions with such beings. The potential discovery of intelligent life or microbial organisms on other celestial bodies prompts complex moral and legal questions about their rights and the obligations of humanity. If we encounter extraterrestrial civilizations, the principles of diplomatic engagement grounded in respect and cohabitation must be enshrined in legal agreements. Mechanisms for dialogue and mutual understanding should drive any interactions, reflecting a shared commitment to coexistence and non-exploitation.

Furthermore, the framework for cosmic exploration must prioritize multilateral cooperation and collaborative research efforts. Given the expansive nature of the universe, no single nation will possess all the resources or technological capabilities necessary for intergalactic travel. Establishing legal agreements that promote joint missions and resource sharing can cultivate a spirit of collaboration while reducing the risks of conflict over cosmic territories. Through international coalitions and partnerships, nations can work together to address the challenges of exploration, fostering scientific advancement while ensuring the equitable distribution of benefits derived from shared discoveries.

An equally important aspect of legal frameworks involves the establishment of compliant guidelines for commercial endeavors in space. As private enterprises increasingly engage in space exploration and potential extraction of resources, there exists a need for regulatory oversight to govern these activities. Developing a comprehensive legal infrastructure that ensures compliance, promotes safety, and prevents harmful practices is vital for creating a sustainable model for commercial involvement in cosmic exploration.

The necessity for flexible frameworks cannot be overstated, given the rapidly evolving landscape of space exploration. Legal responses must be adaptive enough to encompass unforeseen challenges, technological advancements, and emerging ethical dilemmas. The increasing intersection of multiple disciplines—ranging from law and ethics to science and technology—calls for interdisciplinary collaboration to craft effective legal responses to the complexities of cosmic exploration.

Moreover, fostering public engagement and awareness surrounding legal frameworks is essential. As space exploration captivates the imagination of humanity, engaging diverse stakeholders—including scientists, ethicists, educators, and the general public—in discussions about cosmic governance can cultivate a sense of shared responsibility. Public dialogues create opportunities to ground legal frameworks in the values and perspectives of global citizens, enriching the discourse surrounding the implications of our journeys beyond Earth.

In summary, the creation of robust legal frameworks for cosmic exploration necessitates a collaborative, interdisciplinary, and adaptive approach. As humanity embarks on intergalactic travel, legal responses must address resource utilization, environmental protection, ethical interactions with extraterrestrial life, and coordinated efforts among nations and private entities. Upholding principles of shared stewardship, cooperation, and responsibility can pave the way for successful and sustainable cosmic endeavors. The legal structures we establish today will shape the future of our cosmic journey, ensuring that explorations among the stars reflect our highest aspirations and collective commitment to the universe and its inhabitants.